MIND IN SOCIETY

The Development
of Higher
Psychological Processes

Portrait of L. S. Vygotsky at age 35

NB Сущность инструм. методики в функционально различном употреблении двух стимулов, но различному определяющих поведение, и в вытекающем отсюда овладении собственн. психол. операцией. Всегда даны 2 стимула, вопрос стоит так:

1. Как запомнить данное S₁ при помощи данного S₂. Первое S₁ – О, S₂ – J.

2. Как направить внимание на S₁O при помощи S₂J.

3. Как репродуцировать первое слово на S₁O через S₂J и т.г.

Fragment of Vygotsky's note first suggesting mediation as the basis of higher psychological processes. ("*NB*. The essence of the instrumental method resides in the functionally different use of two stimuli, which differentially determine behavior; from this results the mastery of one's own psychological operations. Always assuming two stimuli, we must answer the following questions: 1. How does one remember stimulus S_1 with the aid of stimulus S_2 (where S_1 is the object and S_2 is the instrument). 2. How is attention directed to S_1 with the aid of S_2. 3. How is a word associated with S_1 retrieved via S_2 and so on.")

L. S. VYGOTSKY

Mind in Society

The Development of Higher Psychological Processes

Edited by Michael Cole
Vera John-Steiner
Sylvia Scribner
Ellen Souberman

Harvard
University
Press
Cambridge, Massachusetts
London, England
1978

Library of Congress Cataloging in Publication Data

Vygotskiĭ, Lev Semenovich, 1896–1934.
   Mind in society.

   Includes index.
   1. Cognition.   2. Cognition in children.
I. Cole, Michael, 1938–   II. Title.
BF311.V93   1978   155.4'13   77–26023
ISBN 0–674–57628–4

To the memory of

Alexander Romanovich Luria

Editors' Preface

Lev Semyonovich Vygotsky has figured prominently in American psychology since the publication in 1962 of his monograph *Thought and Language*. Five years ago, at the urging of Vygotsky's student Alexander Luria, we agreed to edit a collection of Vygotsky's essays which would reflect the general theoretical enterprise of which the study of the relation between thought and language was one important aspect. Luria made available to us rough translations of two of Vygotsky's works. The first, "Tool and Symbol in Children's Development (1930), had never been published. The second was a translation of a monograph entitled *The History of the Development of Higher Psychological Functions*, which appeared in the second volume of Vygotsky's writings published in Moscow in 1960. A cursory study of these essays quickly convinced us that the scope of Vygotsky's work reached considerably beyond *Thought and Language*. Furthermore, we came to believe that the image of Vygotsky as a sort of early neobehaviorist of cognitive development—an impression held by many of our colleagues—was strongly belied by these two works.

We have constructed the first four chapters of this volume from "Tool and Symbol." The fifth chapter summarizes the major theoretical and methodological points made in "Tool and Symbol" and applies them to a classic problem in cognitive psychology, the nature of choice reaction. This chapter was taken from section 3 of *The History of the Development of Higher Psychological Functions*. Chapters 6 and 8 (learning and development, and the developmental precursors of writing) are from a posthumously published collection of essays entitled *Mental Development of Children and the Process of Learning* (1935). Chapter 7, on play, is based on a lecture delivered at the Leningrad Pedagogical Institute in 1933 and published in *Voprosi Psikhologii (Problems of Psychology)* in 1966. Complete references are given in the list of Vygotsky's works that follows the text of this volume.

At several places we have inserted material from additional sources in order to more fully explicate the meaning of the text. In most cases these importations are from sections of *The History of the Development of Higher Psychological Functions* other than the one included here; the rest are taken from other essays which appear in either the 1956 or the 1960 volumes of collected works. In a few cases passages have been taken from the work of Vygotsky's students or collaborators which provide concrete examples of experimental procedures or results which the original text describes with extreme brevity. References to these sources are given in the notes.

In putting separate essays together we have taken significant liberties. The reader will encounter here not a literal translation of Vygotsky but rather our edited translation of Vygotsky, from which we have omitted material that seemed redundant and to which we have added material that seemed to make his points clearer. As other editors have noted, Vygotsky's style is extremely difficult. He wrote copiously and many of his manuscripts have never been properly edited. In addition, during frequent periods of illness he would dictate his papers—a practice which resulted in repetitions and dense or elliptical prose. Gaps in the original manuscripts make them even less accessible now than they might have been at the time they were written. Because proper references were rarely given, we have supplied our best guess as to the exact sources to which Vygotsky referred. The process of tracking down and reading these sources has itself proved a very rewarding enterprise; many of his contemporaries were fascinatingly modern in important respects. We realize that in tampering with the original we may have distorted history; however, we hope that by stating our procedures and by adhering as closely as possible to the principles and content of the work, we have not distorted Vygotsky's meaning.

We owe a special debt to the late Alexander R. Luria for providing an initial translation of much of the material included in chapters 1–5, for tirelessly tracking down references and expanding upon details of experiments, and for reading our manuscript. Chapters 6 and 7 were translated by Martin Lopez-Morillas. Chapter 5 and parts of chapters 1–5 were translated by Michael Cole. We wish to thank James Wertsch for his assistance in translating and interpreting especially difficult passages.

The editing of these writings has occupied us for several years. Working in separate locations, educated in differing intellectual traditions, each team of editors found certain material of special interest. Since there is not one but many issues to be illuminated by such a complex body of thought, we have written two essays reflecting various aspects of "reading Vygotsky."

Vera John-Steiner
Ellen Souberman
University of New Mexico

Michael Cole
Sylvia Scribner
The Rockefeller University

Contents

The spider carries out operations reminiscent of a weaver and the boxes which bees build in the sky could disgrace the work of many architects. But even the worst architect differs from the most able bee from the very outset in that before he builds a box out of boards he has already constructed it in his head. At the end of the work process he obtains a result which already existed in his mind before he began to build. The architect not only changes the form given to him by nature, within the constraints imposed by nature, he also carries out a purpose of his own which defines the means and the character of the activity to which he must subordinate his will.

Karl Marx, *Capital*

It is precisely *the alteration of nature by men,* not nature as such, which is the most essential and immediate basis of human thought.

Friedrich Engels, *Dialectics of Nature*

Introduction

MICHAEL COLE AND SYLVIA SCRIBNER

Educated as a lawyer and philologist, Lev S. Vygotsky had already made several contributions to literary criticism when he began his career as a psychologist following the Russian Revolution in 1917. He was a student in the heyday of Wilhelm Wundt, the founder of experimental psychology, and William James, the American pragmatist. His scientific contemporaries included Ivan Pavlov, Vladimir Bekhterev, and John B. Watson, popularizers of stimulus-response theories of behavior, as well as Wertheimer, Köhler, Koffka, and Lewin, the founders of the Gestalt psychology movement. The reader might expect, then, that Vygotsky's work will prove to be primarily of historical interest—perhaps as a glimpse of the way in which modern psychology's founding fathers influenced Soviet psychology in postrevolutionary Russia. These essays are certainly of interest from the perspective of intellectual history, but they are not historical relics. Rather, we offer them as a contribution to quandaries and discussions in contemporary psychology.

In order to understand how the ideas in this volume can retain their relevance across the reaches of time and culture that separate us from Vygotsky, we have repeatedly found ourselves reflecting upon the state of European psychology which provided the initial setting for Vygotsky's theories. We have also found it helpful to examine the condition of psychology and society in postrevolutionary Russia, since they were the source of the immediate problems facing Vygotsky as well as a source of inspiration as he and his colleagues sought to develop a Marxist theory of human intellectual functioning.

NINETEENTH-CENTURY BEGINNINGS

Until the latter half of the nineteenth century the study of man's nature was the province of philosophy. The intellectual descendants of John Locke in England had developed his empiricist explanation of mind, which emphasized the origin of ideas from environmentally produced sensations. The major problem of psychological analysis for these British empiricists was to describe the laws of association by which simple sensations combine to produce complex ideas. On the continent the followers of Immanuel Kant argued that ideas of space and time and concepts of quantity, quality, and relation originate in the human mind and cannot be decomposed into simpler elements. Neither side budged from its armchair. Both of these philosophical traditions were operating under the assumption, dating from the work of René Descartes, that the scientific study of man could apply only to his physical body. To philosophy was assigned the study of his soul.

While the conflict between these two approaches reaches down to the present day, in the 1860s the terms of this discussion were changed irrevocably by the almost simultaneous publication of three books. Most famous was Darwin's *Origin of Species,* which argued the essential continuity of man and other animals. One immediate consequence of this assertion was an effort by many scholars to establish discontinuities that set human adults off from their lower relatives (both ontogenetically and phylogenetically). The second book was Gustav Fechner's *Die Psychophysik,* which provided a detailed, mathematically sophisticated description of the relation between changes in specifiable physical events and verbalizable "psychic" responses. Fechner claimed no less than an objective, quantitative description of the contents of the human mind. The third book was a slim volume entitled *Reflexes of the Brain,* written by a Moscow physician, I. M. Sechenov. Sechenov, who had studied with some of Europe's leading physiologists, had advanced understanding of simple sensory-motor reflexes by using techniques that isolated nerve–muscle preparations from the living organism. Sechenov was convinced that the processes he observed in the isolated tissue of frogs were the same in principle as those that take place in the central nervous systems of intact organisms, including humans. If responses of leg muscles could be accounted for by processes of inhibition and excitation, might not the same laws apply to the operations of the human cerebral cortex? Although he lacked direct evidence for these speculations, Sechenov's ideas suggested the physiological basis for linking the natural scientific study of animals with the heretofore philosophical study of humans. The tsar's censor seemed to understand the revolutionary, materialist implications of Sechenov's thesis; he banned publication of the book for as long as he could. When the book appeared, it bore a dedication to Charles Darwin.

These books by Darwin, Fechner, and Sechenov can be viewed as essential constituents of psychological thought at the end of the nineteenth century. Darwin linked animals and humans in a single conceptual system regulated by natural laws; Fechner provided an example of what a natural law describing the relationship between physical events and human mental functioning might look like; Sechenov, extrapolating from muscle twitches in frogs, proposed a physiological theory of how such mental processes worked within the normally functioning individual. None of these authors considered themselves (or were considered by their contemporaries) to be psychologists. But they provided the central questions with which the young science of psychology became concerned in the second half of the century: What are the relationships between animal and human behavior? Environmental and mental events? Physiological and psychological processes? Various schools of psychology attacked one or another of these questions, providing partial answers within theoretically limited perspectives.

The first such school was established by Wilhelm Wundt in 1880. Wundt took as his task the description of the contents of human consciousness and their relation to external stimulation. His method consisted of analyzing various states of consciousness into their constituent elements, which he defined as simple sensations. On a priori grounds, he ruled out such sensations as "feelings of awareness" or "perception of relations" as elements of consciousness, considering these phenomena to be "nothing more than" the by-product of faulty methods of observation (introspection). Indeed, Wundt propounded the explicit view that complex mental functions, or as they were then known, "higher psychological processes" (voluntary remembering and deductive reasoning, for example), could not *in principle* be studied by experimental psychologists. They could only be investigated, he maintained, by historical studies of cultural products such as folktales, customs, and language.

By the beginning of World War I introspective studies of human conscious processes came under attack from two directions. In the United States and Russia psychologists discontented with the controversies surrounding *the* correct introspective descriptions of sensations, and with the sterility of the research this position had produced, renounced the study of consciousness in favor of the study of behavior. Exploiting the potential suggested by Pavlov's study of conditioned reflexes (which built upon Sechenov) and Darwin's assertion of the continuity of man and beast, they opened up many areas of animal and human behavior to scientific study. In one important respect, however, they agreed with their introspective antagonists: their basic strategy was to identify the simple building blocks of human activity (substituting stimulus-response bonds for sensations) and then to specify the rules by which these elements combined to produce more complex phenomena. This strategy led to a concentration on processes shared by animals and humans and, again, to a neglect of higher processes— thought, language, and volitional behavior. The second line of attack on descriptions of the contents of consciousness came from a group of psychologists who objected to the one point upon which Wundt and the behaviorists agreed: the appropriateness of analyzing psychological processes into their basic constituents. This movement, which came to be known as Gestalt psychology, demonstrated that many intellectual phenomena (Köhler's studies with anthropoid apes were an example) and perceptual phenomena (Wertheimer's studies of apparent movement of flickering lights, for example) could not be accounted for in terms of either the basic elements of consciousness postulated by Wundt or simple stimulus-response theories of behavior. The Gestalt psychologists rejected, in principle, the possibility of accounting for complex processes in terms of simple ones.

Such, in great brevity, was the situation in European psychology when Vygotsky first appeared on the scene. The situation was not very different in Russia.

POSTREVOLUTIONARY PSYCHOLOGY IN RUSSIA

In the early decades of the twentieth century psychology in Russia, as in Europe, was torn between contending schools, each of which offered partial explanations of a limited range of phenomena. In 1923 at the first all-Russian psychoneurological congress K. N. Kornilov initiated the first major organizational and intellectual shift in psychology following the revolution. At that time the prestigious Institute of Psychology in Moscow was headed by G. I. Chelpanov, an adherent of Wundt's introspective psychology and a foe of behaviorism. (He had published the sixth edition of his book, *The Mind of Man,* a critique of materialist theories of the mind, in 1917, just before the revolution.) Chelpanov assigned a restricted role to Marxism in psychology, asserting it could help explain the social organization of consciousness but not the properties of individual consciousness. In a talk entitled "Contemporary

Psychology and Marxism" Kornilov criticized Chelpanov both for the idealistic basis of his psychological theory and for the restricted role he assigned to Marxism in psychology. Kornilov, who called his own approach reactology, sought to subsume all branches of psychology within a Marxist framework that used behavioral reactions as the basic data.

Kornilov's critique of Chelpanov in 1923 won the day. Chelpanov was removed as director of the Institute of Psychology and was replaced by Kornilov, who immediately brought together a corps of young scientists dedicated to formulating and promoting a behavioral, Marxist theory of psychology. Vygotsky must have produced quite a sensation one year later at the second psychoneurological meeting when he gave a talk entitled "Consciousness as an Object of the Psychology of Behavior." Whatever else one extracted from Kornilov's reactological approach, it quite clearly did not feature the role of consciousness in human activity, nor did it accord the concept of consciousness a role in psychological science.[1]

Vygotsky was dissenting from newly established authority. He was not, however, promoting a return to the position advocated by Chelpanov. In his initial speech and a series of subsequent publications, he made it clear that in his view none of the existing schools of psychology provided a firm foundation for establishing a unified theory of human psychological processes. Borrowing a phrase from his German contemporaries, he often referred to the "crisis in psychology" and set himself the task of achieving a synthesis of contending views on a completely new theoretical basis.

For Vygotsky's Gestalt contemporaries, a crisis existed because established theories (primarily Wundt's and Watsonian behaviorism) could not, in their view, explain complex perceptual and problem-solving behaviors. For Vygotsky, the crisis went much deeper. He shared the Gestalt psychologists' dissatisfaction with psychological analysis that began by reducing all phenomena to a set of psychological "atoms." But he felt that the Gestalt psychologists failed to move beyond the description of complex phenomena to the explanation of them. Even if one were to accept the Gestalt criticisms of previous approaches, a crisis would still exist because psychology would remain split into two irreconcilable halves: a "natural science" branch that could explain elementary sensory and reflex processes, and a "mental science" half that could describe emergent properties of higher psychological processes. What Vygotsky sought was a comprehensive approach that would make possible description *and* explanation of higher psychological functions in terms acceptable to natural science. To Vygotsky, explanation meant a great deal. It included identification of the brain mechanisms underlying a particular function; it included a detailed explication of their developmental history to establish the relation between simple and complex forms of what appeared to be the same behavior; and, importantly, it included specification of the societal context in which the behavior developed. Vygotsky's goals were extremely ambitious, perhaps unreasonably so. He did not achieve these goals (as he was well aware). But he did succeed in providing us with an astute and prescient analysis of modern psychology.

A major reason for the continued relevance of Vygotsky's work is that in 1924 and the following decade he constructed a penetrating critique of the notion that an understanding of the higher psychological functions in humans can be found by a multiplication and complication of principles derived from animal psychology, in particular those principles that represent the mechanical combination of stimulus-response laws. At the same time he provided a devastating critique of theories which claim that the properties of adult intellectual functions arise from maturation alone, or are in any way preformed in the child and simply waiting for an opportunity to manifest themselves.

In stressing the social origins of language and thinking, Vygotsky was following the lead of influential French sociologists, but to our knowledge he was the first modern psychologist to suggest the mechanisms by which culture becomes a part of each person's nature. Insisting that psychological functions are a product of the brain's activity, he became an early advocate of combining experimental cognitive psychology with neurology and physiology. Finally, by claiming that all of these should be understood in terms of a Marxist theory of the history of human society, he laid the foundation for a unified behavioral science.

MARXIST THEORETICAL FRAMEWORK

Contrary to the stereotype of Soviet scholars scurrying to make their theories conform to the Politburo's most recent interpretation of Marxism, Vygotsky clearly viewed Marxist thought as a valuable scientific resource from very early in his career. "A psychologically relevant application of dialectical and historical materialism" would be one accurate summary of Vygotsky's sociocultural theory of higher mental processes.

Vygotsky saw in the methods and principles of dialectical materialism a solution to key scientific paradoxes facing his contemporaries. A central tenet of this method is that all phenomena be studied as processes in motion and in change. In terms of the subject matter of psychology, the scientist's task is to reconstruct the origin and course of development of behavior and consciousness. Not only does every phenomenon have its history, but this history is characterized by changes both qualitative (changes in form and structure and basic characteristics) and quantitative. Vygotsky applied this line of reasoning to explain the transformation of elementary psychological processes into complex ones. The schism between natural scientific studies of elementary processes and speculative reflection on cultural forms of behavior might be bridged by tracing the qualitative changes in behavior occuring in the course of development. Thus, when Vygotsky speaks of his approach as "developmental," this is not to be confused with a theory of child development. The developmental method, in Vygotsky's view, is the central method of psychological science.

Marx's theory of society (known as historical materialism) also played a fundamental role in Vygotsky's thinking. According to Marx, historical changes in society and material life produce changes in "human nature" (consciousness and behavior). Although this general proposition had been echoed by others, Vygotsky was the first to attempt to relate it to concrete psychological questions. In this effort he creatively elaborated on Engels' concept of human labor and tool use as the means by which man changes nature and, in so doing, transforms himself. In chapters 1 through 4 below, Vygotsky exploits the concept of a tool in a fashion that finds its direct antecedents in Engels: "The specialization of the hand—this implies the *tool,* and the tool implies specific human activity, the transforming reaction of man on nature";[2] "the animal merely *uses* external nature, and brings about changes in it simply by his presence; man, by his changes, makes it serve his ends, *masters it.* This is the final, essential distinction between man and other animals" (p. 291). Vygotsky brilliantly extended this concept of mediation in human–environment interaction to the use of signs as well as tools. Like tool systems, sign systems (language, writing, number systems) are created by societies over the course of human history and change with the form of society and the level of its cultural development. Vygotsky believed that the internalization of culturally produced sign systems brings about behavioral transformations and forms the bridge between early and later forms of individual development. Thus for Vygotsky, in the tradition of Marx and Engels, the mechanism of individual developmental change is rooted in society and culture.

In later chapters (especially chapter 5) Vygotsky generalizes his conception of the origin of higher psychological functions in a way that reveals the close relationship between their fundamentally mediated nature and the dialectical, materialist conception of historical change.

Citations of Marxist classics were sometimes used to excess by certain Soviet psychologists as they sought a means for building a Marxist psychology from the chaos of competing schools of thought. Yet in unpublished notes Vygotsky repudiated the "quotation method" of relating Marxism to psychology and made explicit the way in which he thought its basic methodological principles might contribute to theory-building in psychology:

> I don't want to discover the nature of mind by patching together a lot of quotations. I want to find out how science has to be built, to approach the study of the mind having learned the whole of Marx's *method*. . . . In order to create such an enabling theory-method in the generally accepted scientific manner, it is necessary to discover the essence of the given area of phenomena, the laws according to which they change, their qualitative and quantitative characteristics, their causes. It is necessary to formulate the categories and concepts that are specifically relevant to them—in other words, to create one's own *Capital*.
>
> The whole of *Capital* is written according to the following method: Marx analyzes a single living "cell" of capitalist society—for example, the nature of value. Within this cell he discovers the structure of the entire system and all of its economic institutions. He says that to a layman this analysis may seem a murky tangle of tiny details. Indeed, there may be tiny details, but they are exactly those which are essential to "micro-anatomy." Anyone who could discover what a "psychological" cell is— the mechanism producing even a single response—would thereby find the key to psychology as a whole. [from unpublished notebooks]

A careful reading of this manuscript provides convincing proof of both Vygotsky's sincerity and the fruitfulness of the framework he developed.

THE INTELLECTUAL AND SOCIAL SETTING

Developmental and historical approaches to the study of human nature were not unique to Vygotsky in the Soviet Union in the 1920s. Within psychology, an older colleague, P. P. Blonsky, had already adopted the position that an understanding of complex mental functions requires developmental analysis.[3] From Blonsky Vygotsky adopted the notion that "behavior can be understood only as the history of behavior." Blonsky was also an early advocate of the view that the technological activities of people were a key to understanding their psychological makeup, a view that Vygotsky exploited in great detail.

Vygotsky and many other Soviet theorists of the day were also heavily influenced by the work of western European sociologists and anthropologists, like Thurnwald and Levy-Bruhl,[4] who were interested in the history of mental processes as reconstructed from anthropological evidence of the intellectual activity of primitive peoples. The scant references in this book are a pale reflection of the extent of Vygotsky's interest in the development of mental processes understood historically. This aspect of his work received special attention in a publication titled *Studies in the History of Behavior* published jointly with A. R. Luria in 1930. It served as the impetus for Luria's two expeditions to Central Asia in 1931 and 1932, the results of which were published long after Vygotsky's death.[5]

This historical emphasis was also popular in Soviet linguistics, where interest centered on the problem of the origin of language and its influence on the development of thought. Discussions in linguistics dealt with concepts similar to Vygotsky's and also similar to the work of Sapir and Whorf, who were then becoming influential in the United States.

While an acquaintance with academic issues of the 1930s is helpful to understanding Vygotsky's approach to human cognition, a consideration of sociopolitical conditions during this time in the Soviet Union is essential as well. Vygotsky worked within a society that put a premium on science and had high hopes for the ability of science to solve the pressing economic and social problems of the Soviet people. Psychological theory could not be pursued apart from the practical demands made on scientists by the government, and the broad spectrum of Vygotsky's work clearly shows his concern with producing a psychology that would have relevance for education and medical practice. For Vygotsky, the need to carry on theoretical work in an applied context posed no contradiction whatsoever. He had begun his career as a teacher of literature, and many of his early articles had dealt with problems of educational practice, especially education of the mentally and physically handicapped. He had been a founder of the Institute of Defectology in Moscow, with which he was associated throughout his working life. In such medical problems as congenital blindness, aphasia, and severe mental retardation Vygotsky saw opportunities both for understanding the mental processes of all people and for establishing programs of treatment and remediation. Thus, it was consistent with his general theoretical view that his work should be carried out in a society that sought the elimination of illiteracy and the founding of educational programs to maximize the potential of individual children.

Vygotsky's participation in the debates surrounding the formulation of a Marxist psychology embroiled him in fierce disputes in the late 1920s and early 1930s. In these discussions ideology, psychology, and policy were intricately intertwined, as different groups vied for the right to represent psychology. With Kornilov's ouster from the Institute of Psychology in 1930, Vygotsky and his students were for a brief time in the ascendancy, but he was never recognized as the official leader.

In the years just prior to his death Vygotsky lectured and wrote extensively on problems of education, often using the term "pedology," which roughly translates as "educational psychology." In general he was scornful of pedology that emphasized tests of intellectual ability patterned after the IQ tests then gaining prominence in western Europe and the United States. It was his ambition to reform pedology along the lines suggested in chapter 6 in this volume, but his ambition far exceeded his grasp. Vygotsky was mistakenly accused of advocating mass psychological testing and criticized as a "Great Russian chauvinist" for suggesting that nonliterate peoples (such as those living in nonindustrialized sections of central Asia) had not yet developed the intellectual capacities associated with modern civilization. Two years following his death the Central Committee of the Communist Party issued a decree halting all psychological testing in the Soviet Union. At the same time all leading psychological journals ceased publication for almost twenty years. A period of intellectual ferment and experimentation was at an end.

But by no means did Vygotsky's ideas die with him. Even before his death he and his students established a laboratory in Kharkov headed by A. N. Leontiev (currently Dean of the Psychology Faculty at Moscow University) and later by A. V. Zaporozhets (now Director of the Institute of Preschool Education). Luria completed his medical training in the latter half of the 1930s and went on to carry out his world-famous pioneering work in developmental and neuropsychology. Many of Vygotsky's former students hold leading positions in the Institute of Defectology and the Institute of Psychology within the Soviet Academy of Pedagogical Sciences, as well as university departments of psychology such as that at Moscow University.

As inspection of any compendium of Soviet psychological research will show, Vygotsky continued and continues to influence research in a wide variety of basic and applied areas related to cognitive processes, their development and dissolution. His ideas have not gone unchallenged, even by his students, but they remain a living part of Soviet psychological thought.

VYGOTSKY'S USE OF THE EXPERIMENTAL METHOD

Vygotsky's references in the text to experiments conducted in his laboratory sometimes leave readers with a sense of unease. He presents almost no raw data and summaries are quite general. Where are the statistical tests that record whether or not observations reflect "real" effects? What do these studies prove? Do they in fact lend any support to Vygotsky's general theories, or is he, in spite of his disclaimers, conducting psychology in a speculative manner without subjecting his central propositions to empirical test? Those steeped in the methodology of experimental psychology as practiced in most American laboratories may be inclined to withhold the term "experiment" from Vygotsky's studies and consider them to be little more than interesting demonstrations or pilot studies. And so, in many respects, they were.

We have found it useful to keep in mind the nature of the manuscripts that are the basis of this book. They do not constitute a report of a series of research studies from which general propositions are extrapolated. Rather, in these writings Vygotsky was concerned with presenting the basic principles of his theory and method. He drew upon the very limited pool of empirical work available to him in order to illustrate and support these principles. The description of specific studies is schematic and findings are often given as general conclusions rather than as raw data. Some of the studies referred to have been published in greater detail by his students and a few are available in English.[6] Most studies, however, were conducted by students as pilot investigations and were never prepared for publication. Vygotsky's laboratory existed for only a decade and his death from tuberculosis was expected at any time. The implications of his theory were so many and varied, and time was so short, that all energy was concentrated on opening up new lines of investigation rather than pursuing any particular line to the fullest. That task remained for Vygotsky's students and their successors, who adopted his views in varying ways, incorporating them into new lines of research.[7] However, the style of experimentation in these essays represents more than a response to the urgent conditions in which they were conducted. Vygotsky's concept of the experiment differed from that of American psychology, and understanding this difference is important for an appreciation of Vygotsky's contribution to contemporary cognitive psychology.

As every student of an introductory experimental course knows, the purpose of an experiment as conventionally presented is to determine the conditions controlling behavior. Methodology follows from this objective: the experimental hypothesis predicts aspects of the stimulus materials or task that will determine particular aspects of the response; the experimenter seeks maximum control over materials, task, and response in order to test the prediction. Quantification of responses provides the basis for comparison across experiments and for drawing inferences about cause-and-effect relationships. The experiment, in short, is designed to produce a certain performance under conditions that maximize its interpretability.

For Vygotsky, the object of experimentation is quite different. The principles of his basic approach (presented in chapter 5 of this volume) do not stem from a purely methodological critique of established experimental practices; they flow from his theory of the nature of higher psychological processes and the task of scientific explanation in psychology. If higher psychological processes arise and undergo changes in the course of learning and development, psychology will only fully understand them by determining their origin and mapping their history. At first sight it would appear that such a task precludes the experimental method and requires study of individual behavior over long periods of time. But Vygotsky believed (and ingeniously demonstrated) that the experiment could serve an important role by making visible processes that are ordinarily hidden beneath the surface of habitual behavior. He wrote that in a properly conceived experiment the investigator could create processes that "telescope the actual course of development of a given function." He called this method of investigation the "experimental-genetic" method, a term he shared with Heinz Werner, an outstanding contemporary whose developmental, comparative approach to psychology was well-known to Vygotsky.

To serve as an effective means of studying "the course of development of process," the experiment must provide maximum opportunity for the subject to engage in a variety of activities that can be observed, not just rigidly controlled. One technique Vygotsky effectively used for this purpose was to introduce obstacles or difficulties into the task that disrupted routine methods of problem solving. For example, in studying children's communication and the function of egocentric speech Vygotsky set up a task situation that required children to engage in cooperative activity with others who did not share their language (foreign-speaking or deaf children). Another method was to provide alternative routes to problem solving, including a variety of materials (Vygotsky called them "external aids") that could be used in different ways to satisfy the demands of the task. By careful observation of the uses made of these external aids by children at different ages under different conditions of task difficulty, Vygotsky sought to reconstruct the series of changes in intellectual operations that normally unfold during the course of the child's biographical development. A third technique was to set a task before the child that exceeded his knowledge and abilities, in order to discover the rudimentary beginnings of new skills. This procedure is well illustrated in studies on writing (chapter 7), in which young toddlers were provided with pencil and paper and asked to make representations of events, thus disclosing to the investigator the child's earliest understanding of the nature of graphic symbolism.

With all these procedures the critical data furnished by the experiment is not performance level as such but the methods by which the performance is achieved. The contrast between conventional experimental work (focusing on performance) and Vygotsky's work (focusing on process) has its contemporary expression in recent studies on children's memory by American investigators. Many studies (including a number of our own) have presented children of various ages with lists of words to be remembered and have analyzed such performance measures as number of words recalled and the order of recall. From these indicators the investigators have sought to make inferences about whether or not, and to what extent, young children engage in organizing activities as a memory strategy. On the other hand, John Flavell and his colleagues, using procedures very much like those of Vygotsky's students, provided children the materials to be remembered, and instructed them to do whatever they wanted to help them remember. They then observed children's attempts at classifying the items, the kinds of grouping they made, and other indices of children's tendency to use organizational strategies in remembering. As with Vygotsky, the central question is: What are the children doing? How are they trying to satisfy task demands?

In this connection we would like to clarify a basic concept of Vygotsky's theoretical approach and experimental method that we believe has been widely misinterpreted. In several places in the text Vygotsky, in referring to the structure of behavior, uses a term that we have translated as "mediated." Occasionally this term is accompanied by a figure depicting a stimulus, a response, and a "mediating link" between them (for example, S-X-R). The same term, and virtually the same diagram, were introduced into American learning theory in the late 1930s and became very popular in the 1950s as attempts were made to extend stimulus-response theories of learning to complex human behavior, especially language. It is important to keep in mind that Vygotsky was not a stimulus-response learning theorist and did not intend his idea of mediated behavior to be thought of in this context. What he did intend to convey by this notion was that in higher forms of human behavior, the individual actively modifies the stimulus situation as a part of the process of responding to it. It was the entire structure of this activity which produced the behavior that Vygotsky attempted to denote by the term "mediating." *somewhat analogous to P. assimil*

Several implications follow from Vygotsky's theoretical approach and method of experimentation. One is that experimental results will be qualitative as well as quantitative in nature. Detailed descriptions, based on careful observation, will constitute an important part of experimental findings. To some, such findings may seem merely anecdotal; Vygotsky maintained that if carried out objectively and with scientific rigor, such observations have the status of validated fact.

Another consequence of this new approach to experimentation is to break down some of the barriers that are traditionally erected between "laboratory" and "field." Experimental interventions and observations may often be as well or better executed in play, school, and clinical settings than in the psychologist's laboratory. The sensitive observations and imaginative interventions reported in this book attest to this possibility.

Finally, an experimental method that seeks to trace the history of the development of psychological functions sits more comfortably than the classical method alongside other methods in the social sciences concerned with history—including the history of culture and society as well as the history of the child. To Vygotsky, anthropological and sociological studies were partners with observation and experiment in the grand enterprise of accounting for the progress of human consciousness and intellect.

Biographical Note on
L. S. Vygotsky

Lev Semyonovitch Vygotsky was born November 5, 1896, in the town of Orsha, northeast of Minsk in Bylorussia. In 1913 he completed gymnasium in Gomel with a gold medal. In 1917, after graduating from Moscow University with a specialization in literature, he began his literary research.

From 1917 to 1923 Vygotsky taught literature and psychology in a school in Gomel, where he also directed the theater section of the adult education center and gave many speeches and lectures on problems of literature and science. During this period Vygotsky founded the literary journal *Verask*. Here he published his first literary research, later reissued as *The Psychology of Art*. He also founded a psychological laboratory in the Teacher Training Institute, where he gave a course on psychology, the contents of which were later published in *Pedagogical Psychology*.

In 1924 Vygotsky moved to Moscow and began to work first at the Institute of Psychology and then in the Institute of Defectology, which he founded. At the same time he directed a department for the education of physically defective and mentally retarded children in Narcompros (Peoples Committee on Education), and taught courses in the Krupkaya Academy of Communist Education, the Second Moscow State University (later the Moscow State Pedagogical Institute), and the Hertzen Pedagogical Institute in Leningrad. Between 1925 and 1934 Vygotsky gathered around him a large group of young scientists working in the areas of psychology, defectology, and mental abnormality. An interest in medicine led Vygotsky simultaneously to undertake medical training, first in the medical institute in Moscow and later in Kharkov, where he gave a psychology course in the Ukrainian Psychoneurological Academy. Not long before his death Vygotsky was invited to head the department of psychology in the All-Union Institute of Experimental Medicine. He died of tuberculosis June 11, 1934.

A. R. Luria

Part One / Mind in Society

Basic Theory and Data

Tool and Symbol in Child Development

The primary purpose of this book is to characterize the uniquely human aspects of behavior, and to offer hypotheses about the way these traits have been formed in the course of human history and the way they develop over an individual's lifetime.

This analysis will be concerned with three fundamental issues: (1) What is the relation between human beings and their environment, both physical and social? (2) What new forms of activity were responsible for establishing labor as the fundamental means of relating humans to nature and what are the psychological consequences of these forms of activity? (3) What is the nature of the relationship between the use of tools and the development of speech? None of these questions has been fully treated by scholars concerned with understanding animal and human psychology.

Karl Stumpf, a prominent German psychologist in the early years of the twentieth century, based his studies on a set of premises completely different from those I will employ here.[1] He compared the study of children to the study of botany, and stressed the botanical character of development, which he associated with maturation of the whole organism.

The fact is that maturation per se is a secondary factor in the development of the most complex, unique forms of human behavior. The development of these behaviors is characterized by complicated, qualitative transformations of one form of behavior into another (or, as Hegel would phrase it, a transformation of quantity into quality). The conception of maturation as a passive process cannot adequately describe these complex phenomena. Nevertheless, as A. Gesell has aptly

19

pointed out, in our approaches to development we continue to use the botanical analogy in our description of child development (for example, we say that the early education of children takes place in a "kindergarten").[2] Recently several psychologists have suggested that this botanical model must be abandoned.

In response to this kind of criticism, modern psychology has ascended the ladder of science by adopting zoological models as the basis for a new general approach to understanding the development of children. Once the captive of botany, child psychology is now mesmerized by zoology. The observations on which these newer models draw come almost entirely from the animal kingdom, and answers to questions about children are sought in experiments carried out on animals. Both the results of experiments with animals and the procedures used to obtain these results are finding their way from the animal laboratory into the nursery.

This convergence of child and animal psychology has contributed significantly to the study of the biological basis of human behavior. Many links between child and animal behavior, particularly in the study of elementary psychological processes, have been established. But a paradox has now emerged. When the botanical model was fashionable, psychologists emphasized the unique character of higher psychological functions and the difficulty of studying them by experimental means. But this zoological approach to the higher intellectual processes—those processes that are uniquely human—has led psychologists to interpret the higher intellectual functions as a direct continuation of corresponding processes in animals. This style of theorizing is particularly apparent in the analysis of practical intelligence in children, the most important aspect of which concerns the child's use of tools.

PRACTICAL INTELLIGENCE IN ANIMALS AND CHILDREN

The work of Wolfgang Köhler is particularly significant in the study of practical intelligence.[3] He conducted many experiments with apes during World War I, and occasionally compared some of his observations of chimpanzees' behavior with particular kinds of responses in children. This direct analogy between practical intelligence in the child and similar response by apes became the guiding principle of experimental work in the field.

K. Buhler's research also sought to establish similarities between child and ape.[4] He studied the way in which young children grasp objects, their ability to make detours while pursuing a goal, and the manner in which they use primitive tools. These observations, as well as his experiment in which a young child is asked to remove a ring from a stick, illustrate an approach akin to Köhler's. Buhler interpreted the manifestations of practical intelligence in children as being of exactly the same type as those we are familiar with in chimpanzees. Indeed, there is a phase in the life of the child that Buhler designated the "chimpanzee age" (p. 48). One ten-month-old infant whom he studied was able to pull a string to obtain a cookie that was attached to it. The ability to remove a ring from a post by lifting it rather than trying to pull it sideways did not appear until the middle of the second year.[5] Although these experiments were interpreted as support for the analogy between the child and apes, they also led Buhler to the important discovery, which will be explicated in later sections, that the beginnings of practical intelligence in the child (he termed it "technical thinking"), as well as the actions of the chimpanzee, are independent of speech.

Charlotte Buhler's detailed observations of infants during their first year of life gave further support to this conclusion.[6] She found the first manifestations of practical intelligence took place at the very young age of six months. However, it is not only tool use that develops at this point in a child's history but also systematic movement and perception, the brain and hands—in fact, the child's entire organism. Consequently, the child's system of activity is determined at each specific stage *both by the child's degree of organic development and by his or her degree of mastery in the use of tools.*

K. Buhler established the developmentally important principle that the beginnings of intelligent speech are preceded by technical thinking, and technical thinking comprises the initial phase of cognitive development. His lead in emphasizing the chimpanzee-like features of children's behavior has been followed by many others. It is in extrapolating this idea that the dangers of zoological models and analogies between human and animal behaviors find their clearest expression. The pitfalls are slight in research that focuses on the preverbal period in the child's development, as Buhler's did. However, he drew a questionable conclusion from his work with very young children when he stated, "The achievements of the chimpanzee are quite independent of language and in the case of man, even in later life, technical thinking, or thinking in terms of tools, is far less closely bound up with language and concepts than other forms of thinking."[7]

Buhler proceeded from the assumption that the relationship between practical intelligence and speech that characterizes the ten-month-old child remains intact throughout her lifetime. This analysis postulating the independence of intelligent action from speech runs contrary to our own findings, which reveal the integration of speech and practical thinking in the course of development.

Shapiro and Gerke offer an important analysis of the development of practical thinking in children based upon experiments modeled after Köhler's problem-solving studies with chimpanzees.[8] They theorize that children's practical thinking is similar to adult thought in certain respects and different in others, and emphasize the dominant role of social experience in human development. In their view, social experience exerts its effect through imitation; when the child imitates the way adults use tools and objects, she masters the very principle involved in a particular activity. They suggest that repeated actions pile up, one upon another, as in a multi-exposure photograph; the common traits become clear and the differences become blurred. The result is a crystalized scheme, a definite principle of activity. The child, as she becomes more experienced, acquires a greater number of models that she understands. These models represent, as it were, a refined cumulative design of all similar actions; at the same time, they are also a rough blueprint for possible types of action in the future.

However, Shapiro and Gerke's notion of adaptation is too firmly linked to a mechanical conception of repetition. For them, social experience serves only to furnish the child with motor schemas; they do not take into account the changes occurring in the internal structure of the child's intellectual operations. In their descriptions of children's problem solving, the authors are forced to note the "specific role fulfilled by speech" in the practical and adaptive efforts of the growing child. But their description of this role is a strange one. "Speech," they say, "replaces and compensates for real adaptation; it does not serve as a bridge leading to past experience but to a purely social adaptation which is achieved via the experimenter." This analysis does not allow for the contribution speech makes to the development of a new structural organization of practical activity.

Guillaume and Meyerson offer a different conclusion regarding the role of speech in the inception of uniquely human forms of behavior.[9] From their extremely interesting experiments on tool use among apes, they concluded that the methods used by apes to accomplish a given task are similar in principle and coincide on certain essential points to those used by people suffering from aphasia (that is, individuals who are deprived of speech). Their findings support my assumption that speech plays an essential role in the organization of higher psychological functions.[10]

These experimental examples bring us full circle to the beginning of our review of psychological theories regarding child development. Buhler's experiments indicate that the practical activity of the young child prior to speech development is identical to that of the ape, and Guillaume and Meyerson suggest that the ape's behavior is akin to that observed in people who are deprived of speech. Both of these lines of work focus our attention on the importance of understanding the practical activity of children at the age when they are just beginning to speak. My own work as well as that of my collaborators is directed at these same problems. But our premises differ from those of previous investigators. Our primary concern is to describe and specify the development of those forms of practical intelligence that are specifically human.

RELATION BETWEEN SPEECH AND TOOL USE

we know this is actually possible.

In his classic experiments with apes Köhler demonstrated the futility of attempting to develop even the most elementary sign and symbolic operations in animals. He concluded that tool use among apes is independent of symbolic activity. Further attempts to cultivate productive speech in the ape have also produced negative results. These experiments showed once more that the purposive behavior of the animal is independent of any speech or sign-using activity.

The study of tool use in isolation from sign use is common in research work on the natural history of practical intellect, and psychologists who studied the development of symbolic processes in the child have followed the same procedure. Consequently, the origin and development of speech, as well as all other sign-using activity, were treated as independent of the organization of the child's practical activity. Psychologists preferred to study the development of sign use as an example of pure intellect and not as the product of the child's developmental history. They often attributed sign use to the child's spontaneous discovery of the relation between signs and their meanings. As W. Stern stated, recognition of the fact that verbal signs have meaning constitutes "the greatest discovery in the child's life."[11] A number of authors fix this happy "moment" at the juncture of the child's first and second year, regarding it as the product of the child's mental activity. Detailed examination of the *development of* speech and other forms of sign use was assumed to be unnecessary. Instead, it has routinely been assumed that the child's mind contains all stages of future intellectual development; they exist in complete form, awaiting the proper moment to emerge.

Not only were speech and practical intelligence assumed to have different origins, but their joint participation in common operations was considered to be of no basic psychological importance (as in the work of Shapiro and Gerke). Even when speech and the use of tools were closely linked in one operation, they were still studied as separate processes belonging to two completely different classes of phenomena. At best, their simultaneous occurrence was considered a consequence of accidental, external factors.

The students of practical intelligence as well as those who study speech development often fail to recognize the interweaving of these two functions. Consequently, the children's adaptive behavior and sign-using activity are treated as parallel phenomena—a view that leads to Piaget's concept of "egocentric" speech.[12] He did not attribute an important role to speech in the organization of the child's activities, nor did he stress its communicative functions, although he was obliged to admit its practical importance.

Although practical intelligence and sign use can operate independently of each other in young children, the dialectical unity of these systems in the human adult is the very essence of complex human behavior. Our analysis accords symbolic activity a specific *organizing* function that penetrates the process of tool use and produces fundamentally new forms of behavior.

SOCIAL INTERACTION AND THE TRANSFORMATION OF PRACTICAL ACTIVITY

Based on the discussion in the previous section, and illustrated by experimental work to be described later, the following conclusion may be made: *the most significant moment in the course of intellectual development, which gives birth to the purely human forms of practical and abstract intelligence, occurs when speech and practical activity, two previously completely independent lines of development, converge.* Although children's use of tools during their preverbal period is comparable to that of apes, as soon as speech and the use of signs are incorporated into any action, the action becomes transformed and organized along entirely new lines. The specifically human use of tools is thus realized, going beyond the more limited use of tools possible among the higher animals.

Prior to mastering his own behavior, the child begins to master his surroundings with the help of speech. This produces new relations with the environment in addition to the new organization of behavior itself. The creation of these uniquely human forms of behavior later produce the intellect and become the basis of productive work: the specifically human form of the use of tools.

Observations of children in an experimental situation similar to that of Köhler's apes show that the children not only *act* in attempting to achieve a goal but also *speak*. As a rule this speech arises spontaneously and continues almost without interruption throughout the experiment. It increases and is more persistent every time the situation becomes more complicated and the goal more difficult to attain. Attempts to block it (as the experiments of my collaborator R. E. Levina have shown) are either futile or lead the child to "freeze up."

Levina posed practical problems for four- and five-year-old children such as obtaining a piece of candy from a cupboard. The candy was placed out of reach so the child could not obtain it directly. As the child got more and more involved in trying to obtain the candy, "egocentric" speech began to manifest itself as part of her active striving. At first this speech consisted of a description and analysis of the situation, but it gradually took on a "planful" character, reflecting possible paths to solution of the problem. Finally, it was included as part of the solution.

For example, a four-and-a-half-year-old girl was asked to get candy from a cupboard with a stool and a stick as possible tools. Levina's description reads as follows: (Stands on a stool, quietly looking, feeling along a shelf with stick.) "On the stool." (Glances at experimenter. Puts stick in other hand.) "Is that really the candy?" (Hesitates.) "I can get it from that other stool, stand and get it." (Gets second stool.) "No, that doesn't get it. I could use the stick." (Takes stick, knocks at the candy.) "It will move now." (Knocks candy.) "It moved, I couldn't get it with the stool, but the, but the stick worked."[13]

In such circumstances it seems both natural and necessary for children to speak while they act; in our research we have found that speech not only accompanies practical activity but also plays a specific role in carrying it out. Our experiments demonstrate two important facts:

(1) A child's speech is as important as the role of action in attaining the goal. Children not only speak about what they are doing; their speech and action are part of *one and the same complex psychological function,* directed toward the solution of the problem at hand.

(2) The more complex the action demanded by the situation and

the less direct its solution, the greater the importance played by speech in the operation as a whole. Sometimes speech becomes of such vital importance that, if not permitted to use it, young children cannot accomplish the given task.

These observations lead me to the conclusion that *children solve practical tasks with the help of their speech, as well as their eyes and hands.* This unity of perception, speech, and action, which ultimately produces internalization of the visual field, constitutes the central subject matter for any analysis of the origin of uniquely human forms of behavior.

To develop the first of these two points, we must ask: What is it that really distinguishes the actions of the speaking child from the actions of an ape when solving practical problems?

The first thing that strikes the experimenter is the incomparably greater *freedom* of children's operations, their greater independence from the structure of the concrete, visual situation. Children, with the aid of speech, create greater possibilities than apes can accomplish through action. One important manifestation of this greater flexibility is that the child is able to ignore the direct line between actor and goal. Instead, he engages in a number of preliminary acts, using what we speak of as instrumental, or mediated (indirect), methods. In the process of solving a task the child is able to include stimuli that do not lie within the immediate visual field. Using words (one class of such stimuli) to create a specific plan, the child achieves a much broader range of activity, applying as *tools* not only those objects that lie near at hand, *but searching for and preparing such stimuli as can be useful in the solution of the task, and planning future actions.*

Second, the practical operations of a child who can speak become much less impulsive and spontaneous than those of the ape. The ape typically makes a series of uncontrolled attempts to solve the given problem. In contrast, the child who uses speech divides the activity into two consecutive parts. She plans how to solve the problem through speech and then carries out the prepared solution through overt activity. Direct manipulation is replaced by a complex psychological process through which inner motivation and intentions, postponed in time, stimulate their own development and realization. This new kind of psychological structure is absent in apes, even in rudimentary forms.

Finally, it is decisively important that speech not only facilitates the child's effective manipulation of objects but also controls *the child's own behavior.* Thus, with the help of speech children, unlike apes, acquire the capacity to be both the subjects and objects of their own behavior.

Experimental investigation of the egocentric speech of children engaged in various activities such as that illustrated by Levina produced the second fact of great importance demonstrated by our experiments: *the relative amount of egocentric speech*, as measured by Piaget's methods, increases in relation to the difficulty of the child's task.[14] On the basis of these experiments my collaborators and I developed the hypothesis that children's egocentric speech should be regarded as the transitional form between external and internal speech. Functionally, egocentric speech is the basis for inner speech, while in its external form it is embedded in communicative speech.

One way to increase the production of egocentric speech is to complicate a task in such a way that the child cannot make direct use of tools for its solution. When faced with such a challenge, the children's emotional use of language increases as well as their efforts to achieve a less automatic, more intelligent solution. They search verbally for a new plan, and their utterances reveal the close connection between egocentric and socialized speech. This is best seen when the experimenter leaves the room or fails to answer the children's appeals for help. Upon being deprived of the opportunity to engage in social speech, children immediately switch over to egocentric speech.

While the interrelationship of these two functions of language is apparent in this setting, it is important to remember that egocentric speech is linked to children's social speech by many transitional forms. The first significant illustration of the link between these two language functions occurs when children find that they are unable to solve a problem by themselves. They then turn to an adult, and verbally describe the method that they cannot carry out by themselves. The greatest change in children's capacity to use language as a problem-solving tool takes place somewhat later in their development, when socialized speech (which has previously been used to address an adult) *is turned inward*. Instead of appealing to the adult, children appeal to themselves; language thus takes on an *intrapersonal function* in addition to its *interpersonal use*. When children develop a method of behavior for guiding themselves that had previously been used in relation to another person, when they organize their own activities according to a social form of behavior, they succeed in applying a social attitude to themselves. The history of the process of *the internalization of social speech* is also the history of the socialization of children's practical intellect.

The relation between speech and action is a dynamic one in the course of children's development. The structural relation can shift even during an experiment. The crucial change occurs as follows: At an early stage speech *accompanies* the child's actions and reflects the vicissitudes of problem solving in a disrupted and chaotic form. At a later stage speech moves more and more toward the starting point of the process, so that it comes to *precede* action. It functions then as an aid to a plan that has been conceived but not yet realized in behavior. An interesting analogy can be found in children's speech while drawing (see also chapter 8). Young children name their drawings only after they have completed them; they need to see them before they can decide what they are. As children get older they can decide in advance what they are going to draw. This displacement of the naming process signifies a change in the function of speech. Initially speech follows actions, is provoked by and dominated by activity. At a later stage, however, when speech is moved to the starting point of an activity, a new relation between word and action emerges. Now speech guides, determines, and dominates the course of action; *the planning function of speech* comes into being in addition to the already existing function of language to reflect the external world.[15]

Just as a mold gives shape to a substance, words can shape an activity into a structure. However, that structure may be changed or reshaped when children learn to use language in ways that allow them to go beyond previous experiences when planning future action. In contrast to the notion of sudden discovery popularized by Stern, we envisage verbal, intellectual activity as a series of stages in which the emotional and communicative functions of speech are expanded by the addition of the planning function. As a result the child acquires the ability to engage in complex operations extending over time.

Unlike the ape, which Köhler tells us is "the slave of its own visual field," children acquire an independence with respect to their concrete surroundings; they cease to act in the immediately given and evident *space*. Once children learn how to use the planning function of their language effectively, their psychological field changes radically. A view of the future is now an integral part of their approaches to their surroundings. In subsequent chapters, I will describe the developmental course of some of these central psychological functions in greater detail.

To summarize what has been said thus far in this section: The specifically human capacity for language enables children to provide for auxiliary tools in the solution of difficult tasks, to overcome impulsive action, to plan a solution to a problem prior to its execution, and to master their own behavior. Signs and words serve children first and foremost as a means of social contact with other people. The cognitive and communicative functions of language then become the basis of a new and superior form of activity in children, distinguishing them from animals.

The changes I have described do not occur in a one-dimensional, even fashion. Our research has shown that very small children solve problems using unique mixtures of processes. In contrast with adults, who react differently to objects and to people, young children are likely to fuse action and speech when responding to both objects and social beings. This fusion of activity is analagous to syncretism in perception, which has been described by many developmental psychologists.

The unevenness I am speaking of is seen quite clearly in a situation where small children, when unable to solve the task before them easily, combine direct attempts to obtain the desired end with a reliance upon emotional speech. At times speech expresses the children's desires, while at other times it serves as a substitute for actually achieving the goal. The child may attempt to solve the task through verbal formulations *and* by appeals to the experimenter for help. This mixture of diverse forms of activity was at first bewildering; but further observations drew our attention to a sequence of actions that clarify the meaning of the children's behavior in such circumstances. For example, after completing a number of intelligent and interrelated actions that should help him solve a particular problem successfully, the child suddenly, upon meeting a difficulty, ceases all attempts and turns for help to the experimenter. Any obstacle to the child's efforts at solving the problem may interrupt his activity. The child's verbal appeal to another person is an effort to fill the hiatus his activity has revealed. By asking a question, the child indicates that he has, in fact, formulated a plan to solve the task before him, but is unable to perform all the necessary operations.

Through repeated experiences of this type, children learn covertly (mentally) to plan their activities. At the same time they enlist the assistance of another person in accordance with the requirements of the problem posed for them. The child's ability to control another person's behavior becomes a necessary part of the child's practical activity.

Initially this problem solving in conjunction with another person is not differentiated with respect to the roles played by the child and his helper; it is a general, syncretic whole. We have more than once observed that in the course of solving a task, children get confused because they begin to merge the logic of what they are doing with the logic of the same problem as it has to be solved with the cooperation of another person. Sometimes syncretic action manifests itself when children realize the hopelessness of their direct efforts to solve a problem. As in the example from Levina's work, children address the objects of their attention equally with words and sticks, demonstrating the fundamental and inseparable tie between speech and action in the child's activity; this unity becomes particularly clear when compared with the separation of these processes in adults.

In summary, children confronted with a problem that is slightly too complicated for them exhibit a complex variety of responses including direct attempts at attaining the goal, the use of tools, speech directed toward the person conducting the experiment or speech that simply accompanies the action, and direct, verbal appeals to the object of attention itself.

If analyzed dynamically, this alloy of speech and action has a very specific function in the history of the child's development; it also demonstrates the logic of its own genesis. From the very first days of the child's development his activities acquire a meaning of their own in a system of social behavior and, being directed towards a definite purpose, are refracted through the prism of the child's environment. The path from object to child and from child to object passes through another person. This complex human structure is the product of a developmental process deeply rooted in the links between individual and social history.

The Development of
Perception and Attention

The linkage between tool use and speech affects several psychological functions, in particular perception, sensory-motor operations, and attention, each of which is part of a dynamic system of behavior. Experimental-developmental research indicates that the connections and relations among functions constitute systems that change as radically in the course of a child's development as do the individual functions themselves. Considering each function in turn, I will examine how speech introduces qualitative changes in both its form and its relation to other functions.

Köhler's work emphasized the importance of the structure of the visual field in organizing the ape's practical behavior. The entire process of problem solving is essentially determined by perception. In this respect Köhler had ample grounds for believing that these animals are bound by their sensory field to a much greater extent than adult humans. They are incapable of modifying their sensory field by means of voluntary effort. Indeed, it would probably be useful to view as a general law the dependence of all natural forms of perception on the structure of the sensory field.

However, a child's perception, because it is *human*, does not develop as a direct continuation and further perfection of the forms of animal perception, not even of those animals that stand nearest to humankind. Experiments conducted to clarify this problem led us to discover some basic laws that characterize the higher human forms of perception.

The first set of experiments concerned developmental stages of picture perception in children. Similar experiments describing specific aspects of young children's perception and its dependence on higher psychological mechanisms had been carried out earlier by Binet and analyzed in detail by Stern.[1] Both authors found that the way small children describe pictures differs at successive developmental stages. A two-year-old usually limits his description to separate objects within the picture. Older children describe actions and indicate the complex relations among the separate objects within the picture. Stern inferred from these observations that a stage when children perceive separate objects precedes the stage when they perceive actions and relations in addition to objects, that is, when they perceive the picture as a whole. However, many psychological observations suggest that the child's perceptual processes are initially fused and only later become more differentiated.

We resolved the contradiction between these two positions through an experiment replicating Stern's study of children's descriptions of pictures, in which we asked children to communicate the contents of a picture without using speech. We suggested that the description be made *in pantomime*. The two-year-old child, who according to Stern's schema is still at the separate "object" stage of development, perceived the dynamic features of the picture and reproduced them with ease through pantomime. What Stern regarded as a characteristic of the child's perceptual skills proved to be a product of the limitations of her *language development* or, in other words, a feature of her *verbalized perception*.

A series of related observations revealed that labeling is the primary function of speech used by young children. Labeling enables the child to choose a specific object, to single it out from the entire situation he is perceiving. Simultaneously, however, the child embellishes his first words with very expressive gestures, which compensate for his difficulties in communicating meaningfully through language. By means of words children single out separate elements, thereby overcoming the natural structure of the sensory field and forming new (artifically introduced and dynamic) structural centers. The child begins to perceive the world not only through his eyes but also through his speech. As a result, the immediacy of "natural" perception is supplanted by a complex mediated process; as such, speech becomes an essential part of the child's cognitive development.

Later, the intellectual mechanisms related to speech acquire a new function; verbalized perception in the child is no longer limited to labeling. At this next stage of development, speech acquires a synthesizing function, which in turn is instrumental in achieving more complex forms of cognitive perception. These changes give human perception an entirely new character, quite distinct from the analogous processes in higher animals.

The role of language in perception is striking because of the opposing tendencies implicit in the nature of visual perception and language. The independent elements in a visual field are simultaneously perceived; in this sense, *visual perception is integral.* Speech, on the other hand, requires sequential processing. Each element is separately labeled and then connected in a sentence structure, *making speech essentially analytical.*

Our research has shown that even at very early stages of development, language and perception are linked. In the solution of nonverbal tasks, even if a problem is solved without a sound being uttered, language plays a role in the outcome. These findings substantiate the thesis of psychological linguistics as formulated many years ago by A. Potebnya, who argued for the inevitable interdependence between human thought and language.[2]

A special feature of human perception—which arises at a very young age—is the *perception of real objects.* This is something for which there is no analogy in animal perception. By this term I mean that I do not see the world simply in color and shape but also as a world with sense and meaning. I do not merely see something round and black with two hands; I see a clock and I can distinguish one hand from the other. Some brain-injured patients say, when they see a clock, that they are seeing something round and white with two thin steel strips, but they do not know it is a clock; such people have lost their real relationship with objects. These observations suggest that all human perception consists of categorized rather than isolated perceptions.

The developmental transition to qualitatively new forms of behavior is not confined to changes in perception alone. Perception is part of a dynamic system of behavior; hence, the relation between transformations of perceptual processes and transformations in other intellectual activities is of primary importance. This point is illustrated by our studies on choice behavior, which show the changing relation between perception and motor action in young children.

STUDIES OF CHOICE BEHAVIOR IN CHILDREN

We requested four- and five-year-old children to press one of five keys on a keyboard as they identified each one of a series of picture stimuli assigned to each key. Because this task exceeds the capabilities of the children, it causes serious difficulties and more intensive efforts to solve the problem. Perhaps the most remarkable result is that the entire process of selection by the child is *external,* and concentrated in the motor sphere, thus allowing the experimenter to observe the very nature of the choice process itself in the child's movements. The child does her selecting while carrying out whatever movements the choice requires.

The structure of the child's decision does not in the least resemble the adult process. Adults make a preliminary decision internally and subsequently carry out the choice in the form of a single movement that executes the plan. The child's choice resembles a somewhat delayed *selection among his own movements.* Vascillations in perception are directly reflected in the structure of movement. The child's movements are replete with diffuse gropings that interrupt and succeed one another. A mere glance at the chart tracing the child's movements is sufficient to convince one of the basic motor nature of the process.

The main difference between the choice processes in the child and in the adult is that for the child the series of tentative movements constitute the selection process. The child does not choose the *stimulus* (the necessary key) as the starting point for the consequent movement but rather selects the *movement,* using the instruction as a guide to check the results. Thus, the child resolves her choice not through a direct process of visual perception but through movement, hesitating between two stimuli, her fingers hovering above and moving from one key to another, going half-way and then coming back. When the child transfers her attention to a new location, thereby creating a new focus in the dynamic structure of perception, her hand obediently moves toward this new center, in unison with the eye. In short, movement is not separated from perception: the processes coincide almost exactly.

In the behavior of the higher animals, visual perception forms part of a more complex whole in a similar way. The ape does not perceive the visual situation passively; a complex behavioral structure consisting of reflexive, affective, motor, and intellectual factors is directed toward acquiring the object that attracts it. The ape's movements constitute an immediate dynamic continuation of its perception. In human children, this early, diffusely structured response undergoes a fundamental change as soon as a more complex psychological function is utilized in the choice process. The natural process present in animals is then transformed into a higher psychological operation.

Subsequent to the experiment described above we attempted to simplify the task of selection by marking each key with a corresponding sign to serve as an additional stimulus that could direct and organize the choice process. The child was asked, upon the appearance of a target stimulus, to press the key marked with the corresponding sign. As early as age five or six the child is able to fulfill this task easily. The addition of this new ingredient radically changes the structure of the choice process. The elementary, "natural" operation is replaced by a new and more complicated one. The simpler task evokes a more complexly structured response. When the child attends to the auxiliary sign in order to find the key corresponding to the given stimulus, he no longer exhibits those motor impulses that arise directly from perception. There are no uncertain groping movements in the air such as we observed in the earlier choice reaction when auxiliary aids were not used.

The use of auxiliary signs breaks up the fusion of the sensory field and the motor system and thus makes new kinds of behavior possible. A "functional barrier" is created between the initial and final moments of the choice response; the direct impulse to move is shunted by preliminary circuits. The child who formerly solved the problem impulsively now solves it through an internally established connection between the stimulus and the corresponding auxiliary sign. The movement that previously had been the choice now serves only to fulfill the prepared operation. *The system of signs restructures the whole psychological process and enables the child to master her movement. It reconstructs the choice process on a totally new basis.* Movement detaches itself from direct perception and comes under the control of sign functions included in the choice response. This development represents a fundamental break with the natural history of behavior and initiates the transition from the primitive behavior of animals to the higher intellectual activities of humans.

Attention should be given first place among the major functions in the psychological structure underlying the use of tools. Beginning with Köhler, scholars have noted that the ability or inability to direct one's attention is an essential determinant of the success or failure of any practical operation. However, the difference between the practical intelligence of children and animals is that children are capable of reconstructing their perception and thus freeing themselves from the given structure of the field. With the help of the indicative function of words, the child begins to master his attention, creating new structural centers in the perceived situation. As K. Koffka so aptly put it, the child is able to determine for herself the "center of gravity" of her perceptual field; her behavior is not regulated solely by the salience of individual elements within it. The child evaluates the relative importance of these elements, singling out new "figures" from the background and thus widening the possibilities for controlling her activities.[3]

In addition to reorganizing the visual-spatial field, the child, with the help of speech, creates a time field that is just as perceptible and real to him as the visual one. The speaking child has the ability to direct his attention in a dynamic way. He can view changes in his immediate situation from the point of view of past activities, and he can act in the present from the viewpoint of the future.

For the ape, the task is unsolvable unless the goal and the object needed to reach it are both simultaneously in view. For the child, this gap is easily overcome by verbally controlling her attention and thereby reorganizing her perceptual field. The ape will perceive a stick one moment, but cease to pay attention to it after its visual field has changed and the goal comes into view. The ape must see his stick in order to pay attention to it; the child may pay attention in order to see.

Thus, the child's field of attention embraces not one but a whole series of potential perceptual fields that form successive, dynamic structures over time. The transition from the simultaneous structure of the visual field to the successive structure of the dynamic field of attention is achieved through the reconstruction of the separate activities that are a part of the required operations. When this occurs, we can say that the field of attention has detached itself from the perceptual field and unfolded itself in time, as one component of a dynamic series of psychological activities.

The possibility of combining elements of the past and present visual fields (for instance, tool and goal) in one field of attention leads in turn to a basic reconstruction of another vital function, *memory*. (See chapter 3.) Through verbal formulations of past situations and activities, the child frees himself from the limitations of direct recall; he succeeds in synthesizing the past and present to suit his purposes. The changes that occur in memory are similar to those that occur in the child's perceptual field where centers of gravity are shifted and figure and ground relationship are altered. The child's memory not only makes fragments of the past more available, but also results in a *new method of uniting the elements of past experience with the present.*

Created with the help of speech, the time field for action extends both forward and backward. Future activity that can be included in an ongoing activity is represented by signs. As in the case of memory and attention, the inclusion of signs in temporal perception does not lead to a simple lengthening of the operation in time; rather, it creates the conditions for the development of a single system that includes effective elements of the past, present, and future. This emerging psychological system in the child now encompasses two new functions: *intentions and symbolic representations of purposeful action.*

This change in the structure of the child's behavior is related to basic alterations in the child's needs and motivations. When Lindner compared the methods by which deaf children solved tasks to the methods used by Köhler's ape, he noted that the motives guiding the ape and those guiding the child to achieve mastery of a goal were not the same.[4] The "instinctive" urges predominating in the animal become secondary in the child. New motives, socially rooted and intense, provide the child with direction. K. Lewin described these motives as *Quasi-Beduerfnisse* (quasi-needs) and argued that their inclusion in any given task leads to the reorganization of the child's whole affective and voluntary system.[5] He believed that with the development of these quasi-needs, the child's emotional thrust is shifted *from a preoccupation with the outcome* to *the nature of the solution.* In essence, the "task" (*Aufgabe*) in experiments with apes exists only in the eyes of the experimenter; as far as the animal is concerned there exists only the bait and the obstacles standing in his way. The child, however, strives to solve the given problem and thus has an entirely different purpose. Because he is able to form quasi-needs, the child is capable of breaking the operation into its separate parts, each of which becomes an independent problem that he formulates for himself with the help of speech.

In his excellent analysis of the psychology of purposeful activity, Lewin gives a clear-cut definition of voluntary activity as a product of the historical-cultural development of behavior and as a unique feature of human psychology. The fact that man displays extraordinary freedom with respect to even the most senseless intention is astounding in itself, he asserts. This freedom is incomparably less characteristic of children and probably of nonliterate humans, too. There is reason to believe that voluntary activity, more than highly developed intellect, distinguishes humans from the animals which stand closest to them.

3

*Mastery of Memory
and Thinking*

In the light of what my collaborators and I had learned about the functions of speech in reorganizing perception and creating new relations among psychological functions, we undertook a broad study of other forms of sign-using activity in children in all its concrete manifestations (drawing pictures, writing, reading, using number systems, and so on). We also considered whether other operations not related to practical intellect would show the same laws of development we had discovered when analyzing practical intellect.

Several series of experiments carried out by my colleagues and myself dealt with these problems, and now, based on the data we obtained from them, we are able to describe in schematic form the basic laws that characterize the structure and development of the child's sign operations. These will be presented through a discussion of memory, which is exceptionally appropriate for study of the changes that signs introduce into basic psychological functions because it clearly reveals the social origin of signs as well as their crucial role in the individual's development,

SOCIAL ORIGINS OF INDIRECT (MEDIATED) MEMORY

A comparative investigation of human memory reveals that, even at the earliest stages of social development, there are two, principally different, types of memory. One, dominating in the behavior of nonliterate peoples, is characterized by the nonmediated impression of materials, by the retention of actual experiences as the basis of mnemonic (memory) traces. We call this *natural memory*, and it is clearly illustrated in E. R. Jaensch's studies of eidetic imagery.[1] This kind of memory is very close to perception, because it arises out of the direct influence of external stimuli upon human beings. From the point of view of structure, the entire process is characterized by a quality of immediacy.

Natural memory is not the only kind, however, even in the case of nonliterate men and women. On the contrary, other types of memory belonging to a completely different developmental line coexist with natural memory. The use of notched sticks and knots,[2] the beginnings of writing and simple memory aids all demonstrate that even at early stages of historical development humans went beyond the limits of the psychological functions given to them by nature and proceeded to a new culturally-elaborated organization of their behavior. Comparative analysis shows that such activity is absent in even the highest species of animals; we believe that these sign operations are the product of specific conditions of *social* development.

Even such comparatively simple operations as tying a knot or marking a stick as a reminder change the psychological structure of the memory process. They extend the operation of memory beyond the biological dimensions of the human nervous system and permit it to incorporate artificial, or self-generated, stimuli, which we call *signs*. This merger, unique to human beings, signifies an entirely new form of behavior. The essential difference between it and the elementary functions is to be found in the structure of the stimulus-response relations of each. The central characteristic of elementary functions is that they are totally and directly determined by stimulation from the environment. For higher functions, the central feature is self-generated stimulation, that is, the creation and use of artificial stimuli which become the immediate causes of behavior.

STRUCTURE OF SIGN OPERATIONS

Every elementary form of behavior presupposes a *direct* reaction to the task set before the organism (which can be expressed by the simple S———→R formula). But the structure of sign operations requires an intermediate link between the stimulus and the response. This intermediate link is a second order stimulus (sign) that is drawn into the operation where it fulfills a special function; it creates a new relation between S and R. The term "drawn into" indicates that an individual must be actively engaged in establishing such a link. This sign also possesses the important characteristic of reverse action (that is, it operates on the individual, not the environment).

Consequently, the simple stimulus-response process is replaced by a complex, mediated act, which we picture as:

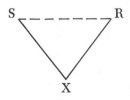

Figure 1

In this new process the direct impulse to react is inhibited, and an auxiliary stimulus that facilitates the completion of the operation by indirect means is incorporated.

Careful studies demonstrate that this type of organization is basic to all higher psychological processes, although in much more sophisticated forms than that shown above. The intermediate link in this formula is not simply a method of improving the previously existing operation, nor is it a mere additional link in an S–R chain. Because this auxiliary stimulus possesses the specific function of reverse action, it transfers the psychological operation to higher and qualitatively new forms and permits humans, by the aid of extrinsic stimuli, *to control their behavior from the outside*. The use of signs leads humans to a specific structure of behavior that breaks away from biological development and creates new forms of a culturally-based psychological process.

EARLY SIGN OPERATIONS IN CHILDREN

The following experiments, conducted under A. N. Leontiev in our laboratories, demonstrate with particular clarity the role of signs in voluntary attention and memory.[3]

Children were asked to play a game in which they were to answer a set of questions without using certain words in their answers. As a rule each child was presented three or four tasks differing in the constraints placed upon answers and the kinds of potential stimulus aids the child could use. In each task the child was asked eighteen questions, seven of which had to do with color (for example, "What color is . . . ?"). The child was asked to answer each question promptly using a single word. The *initial task* was conducted in exactly this fashion. With the *second task*, we began to introduce additional rules that the child had to follow in order to succeed. For example, there were two color names the child was forbidden to use, and no color name could be used twice. The *third task* had the same rules as the second, but the child was given nine colored cards as aids to playing the game ("these cards can help you to win"). The *fourth task* was like the third and was used in cases where the child either failed to use the color cards or began to do so only late in the third task. Before and after each task we asked the child questions to determine if she remembered and understood the instructions.

A set of questions for a typical task is the following (in this case green and yellow are the forbidden colors): (1) Have you a playmate? (2) What color is your shirt? (3) Did you ever go in a train? (4) What color are the railway-carriages? (5) Do you want to be big? (6) Were you ever at the theater? (7) Do you like to play in the room? (8) What color is the floor? (9) And the walls? (10) Can you write? (11) Have you seen lilac? (12) What color is lilac? (13) Do you like sweet things? (14) Were you ever in the country? (15) What colors can leaves be? (16) Can you swim? (17) What is your favorite color? (18) What does one do with a pencil?

For the third and fourth tasks the following color cards were provided as aids: black, white, red, blue, yellow, green, lilac, brown, and gray.

The results for thirty subjects ranging in age from five to twenty-seven years are summarized in table 1, which contains the average number of errors on tasks 2 and 3 and the difference between the two tasks. Looking first at the data from task 2, we see a slight decrease in errors from ages five to thirteen and a sharp drop in adulthood. For task 3 the sharpest drop occurs between the five-to-six and eight-to-nine-year-old groups. The difference between tasks 2 and 3 is small for both

Table 1. Errors on forbidden colors task.

Age	Number of subjects	Errors (average)		Difference
		Task 2	Task 3	
5–6	7	3.9	3.6	0.3
8–9	7	3.3	1.5	1.8
10–13	8	3.1	0.3	2.8
22–27	8	1.4	0.6	0.8

the preschool children and the adults. The difference is largest for the school-age children.

The processes that give rise to the summary figures are most readily revealed by looking at transcripts representative of children in the different groups. The preschool children (age five to six years) were generally unable to discover how to use the auxiliary color cards and had a great deal of trouble with both tasks. Even when we tried to explain to them how the color cards could help them, children at this age were incapable of using these external stimuli in order to organize their own behavior.

The following transcript is from a five-year-old boy:

Task 4. Forbidden colors: blue and red (with cards).

2. What color are houses?	Red [without looking at forbidden colors].
3. Is the sun shining brightly?	Yes.
4. What color is the sky?	White [without looking at card; but after replying, searches for white card]. Here it is! [Picks it up and keeps it in his hand.]
8. What colors are tomatoes?	Red. [Glances at cards.]
9. And what color are exercise books?	White—like this! [pointing to white card].
12. What color are balls?	White [looking at card].
13. Do you live in the town?	No.
. . .	. . .
Do you think you have won?	Don't know—yes.
What must you not do if you want to win?	Mustn't say red or blue.
And what else?	Mustn't say the same word twice.

This transcript suggests that the "aids" actually hindered this child. His repeated use of "white" as a response occurred when his attention was fixed on the white card. The aids are only an accidental feature of the situation for him. Still, there is no doubt that preschool children sometimes demonstrate precursors of the use of external signs. From this point of view certain cases are of special interest. For example, after we suggested to a child that he use the cards to carry out his task ("take the cards, they will help you to win"), he searched for the forbidden colors and put all such cards out of his sight, as if trying to prevent himself from naming them.

In spite of their apparent variety, methods for using the cards can be reduced to two basic types. First the child may put forbidden colors out of sight, display the remainder, and, as he answers the questions, place the colors already named to one side. This is the less effective but the earliest method used. The card in this case serves only to register the named color. Initially, children often do not turn to the cards before they answer the question about color, and only after it is named do they search among the cards, turn over, move, or put away the one named. This is undoubtedly the simplest act of memorization with the help of external means. It is only later that the conditions of the experiment bestow a new, second function on the cards. Before naming a color the child makes a selection with the help of the cards. It makes no difference whether the child looks at the cards so far unused or whether she attends to the colors she has already named. In either case the cards are interposed in the process and serve as a means of regulating her activity. The preliminary hiding of forbidden colors, which is a distinguishing characteristic of the first method for using the cards, does not yet lead to the complete substitution of a less mature operation by a more complex one; it represents merely a step in that direction. Its occurrence is explained partly by the greater simplicity of this operation in mastering memory and partly by a "magical" attitude toward various potential problem-solving aids that children frequently display.

The following examples from a thirteen-year-old schoolgirl illustrate these points:

Task 2. Forbidden colors: green and yellow (without cards).

1.	Have you playmates?	Yes.
2.	What color is your blouse?	Gray.
3.	Have you been in a train?	Yes.
4.	What color are railway carriages?	Gray. [Notices that she has repeated the same color twice, laughs.]
5.	Do you want to be a big girl?	Yes.
6.	Were you ever in a theater?	Yes.
7.	Do you like to play in the room?	Yes.
8.	What color is the floor?	Gray. [Hesitates.] Again—I repeated it.
9.	And the walls?	White.
10.	Can you write?	Yes.
11.	Have you seen lilac?	Yes.
12.	What color is lilac?	Lilac color.
13.	Do you like sweets?	Yes.
14.	Were you ever in the country?	Yes.

Task 2. Forbidden colors: green and yellow (without cards)—cont.

15.	And what color were the leaves?	Green—no, shouldn't have said green—brown, red, sometimes.
16.	Can you swim?	Yes.
17.	What is your favorite color?	Yellow! I can't! [Throws up hands behind head.]
18.	What do you do with a pencil?	Write.
	What do you think, did you win or lose?	Lost.
	What should you not have said?	Green and yellow.
	And what else?	Shouldn't repeat.

Task 3. Forbidden colors: blue and red (with cards).

The subject puts forbidden colors to one side and spreads out the remainder in a row before her.

1.	Do you go for walks in the street?	Yes.
2.	What color are the houses?	Gray. [After answering, looks at the cards and turned over the gray one.]
3.	Is the sun shining brightly?	Brightly.
4.	What color is the sky?	White. [First looks at card and then turns it over.]
5.	Do you like candy?	Yes.
6.	Have you seen a rose?	Yes.
7.	Do you like vegetables?	Yes.
8.	What color are tomatoes?	Green. [Turns over card.]
9.	And exercise books?	Yellow. [Turns over card.]
10.	Have you any toys?	No.
11.	Do you play ball?	Yes.
12.	And what color are balls?	Gray [without glancing at cards; after answering, glances and notices mistake].
13.	Do you live in the town?	Yes.
14.	Did you see the demonstration?	Yes.
15.	What color are flags?	Black. [First looks at cards and then turns one over.]
16.	Have you any books?	Yes.
17.	What colors are their covers?	Lilac [turning over card].
18.	When does it get dark?	At night.

Our results as reflected in the transcripts and table 1 indicate three basic stages in the development of mediated remembering. At the first stage (preschool age) the child is not capable of mastering his behavior by organizing special stimuli. The colored cards that might help the child in his task do not increase to any considerable extent the effectiveness of this operation. Although they act as stimuli, they do not acquire an instrumental function. The second stage of development is characterized by a sharp difference in the indices in both of the main tasks. The introduction of cards as a system of auxiliary, external stimuli raises the effectiveness of the child's activity considerably. At this stage the external sign predominates. The auxiliary stimulus is a psychological instrument acting from the outside. At the third stage (among adults) the difference between their performance in the two tasks decreases and their coefficients become more nearly equal, but now on a new and higher basis. This does not mean that the behavior of adults again becomes direct and natural. At this higher stage of development behavior remains mediated. But now we see that in the third task the auxiliary stimuli are emancipated from primary external forms. What takes place is what we have called internalization; the external sign that school children require has been transformed into an internal sign produced by the adult as a means of remembering. This series of tasks applied to people of different ages shows how the external forms of mediated behavior develop.

THE NATURAL HISTORY OF SIGN OPERATIONS

Although the indirect (or mediated) aspect of psychological operations is an essential feature of higher mental processes, it would be a great mistake, as I pointed out with respect to the beginnings of speech, to believe that indirect operations appear as the result of a pure logic. They are not invented or discovered by the child in the form of a sudden insight or lightning-quick guess (the so-called "aha" reaction). The child does not suddenly and irrevocably deduce the relation between the sign and the method for using it. Nor does she intuitively develop an abstract attitude derived, so to speak, from "the depths of the child's own mind." This metaphysical view, according to which inherent psychological schemata exist prior to any experience, leads inevitably to an a priori conception of higher psychological functions.

Our research has led us to quite different conclusions. We have found that sign operations appear as a result of a complex and prolonged process subject to all the basic laws of psychological evolution. *This means that sign-using activity in children is neither simply invented nor passed down by adults;* rather it arises from something that is originally not a sign operation and becomes one only after a series of *qualitative* transformations. Each of these transformations provides the conditions for the next stage and is itself conditioned by the preceding one; thus, transformations are linked like stages of a single process, and are historical in nature. In this respect, the higher psychological functions are no exception to the general rule that applies to elementary processes; they, too, are subject to the fundamental law of development which knows no exceptions, and appear in the general course of the child's psychological development as the outcome of the same dialectical process, not as something introduced from without or from within.

If we include this history of higher psychological functions as a factor in psychological development, we must arrive at a new concept of development itself. *Within* a general process of development, two qualitatively different lines of development, differing in origin, can be distinguished: the elementary processes, which are of biological origin, on the one hand, and the higher psychological functions, of sociocultural origin, on the other. *The history of child behavior is born from the interweaving of these two lines.* The history of the development of the higher psychological functions is impossible without a study of their prehistory, their biological roots, and their organic disposition. The developmental roots of two fundamental, cultural forms of behavior arise during infancy: the use of *tools* and human *speech.* This alone places infancy at the center of the prehistory of cultural development.

The potential for complex sign operations is embedded in the earliest stages of individual development. However, observations show that between the initial level (elementary behavior) and the higher levels (mediated forms of behavior) many *transitional psychological systems* occur. In the history of behavior these transitional systems lie between the biologically given and the culturally acquired. We refer to this process as *the natural history of the sign.*

Another experimental paradigm designed to study mediated memorizing provides the opportunity to observe this natural history of the sign. N. G. Morozova presented children with words to remember and auxiliary pictures that could be used as mediators.[4] She found that during the preschool years the idea of purposefully using the auxiliary picture (sign) as a means of memorizing is still foreign to the child. Even if the child did turn to the auxiliary picture in order to memorize a given word, it was not necessarily easy for him to execute the reverse operation. At this stage the learner does not usually recall the primary stimulus when being shown the auxiliary stimulus. Rather, the sign evokes a new associative or syncretic series represented by the following scheme:

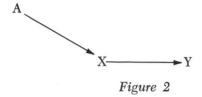

Figure 2

The operation has not yet progressed to the more advanced level which is mediated in form using culturally elaborated features. In contrast with figure 2, the usual scheme for mediated memorizing can be represented by the following:

Figure 3

During the process represented by figure 2, Y *may* lead to a whole series of new associations, among which the subject *may* arrive at the starting point A. However, this sequence is still devoid of its purposeful and instrumental character. In the second scheme, the word's auxiliary sign, X, possesses the quality of reverse action, so that the subject can reliably retrieve A.

The steps leading from the scheme in figure 2 to the scheme in figure 3 can be illustrated by the following examples taken from the work of my students. L. V. Zankov demonstrated that younger children, particularly between the ages of four and six, must rely on meaningful, ready-made links between the "reminder" sign and the word to be remembered.[5] If meaningless figures were presented as memory aids, the children would often refuse to make use of them; they would make no attempt to make up connections between the picture cue and the word they were supposed to remember. Rather, they would attempt to turn these figures into direct copies of the to-be-remembered word.

For example, the figure △ , presented as a reminder of the word "bucket," was turned upside down by the children and served to remind them of the word only when the figure ▽ really began to resemble a bucket. Similarly, the figure ⌂ became the sign of the word "bench" only when turned upside down (⌂). In all these cases, children linked the figures to the word stimuli by changing the meaning of the sign instead of using the mediating link offered by the experimenter. The introduction of these meaningless figures encouraged the children to engage in active mnemonic activity instead of relying on already formed links, but it also led them to treat the sign stimulus as the direct representation of the object to be remembered. When this proved impossible, the child refused to memorize.

A similar phenomenon is apparent in U. C. Yussevich's unpublished study with small children. The auxiliary stimuli, which were pictures that bore no direct relation to the word presented, were rarely used as signs. The child looked at the picture and tried to see in it the object she had to remember. For example, when asked to remember the word "sun" with the help of a picture showing an axe, one child did it very easily; she pointed to a small yellow spot in the drawing and said, "There it is, the sun." This child replaced potentially complex instrumental memorization by a search for a direct representation of the stimulus (akin to an eidetic image). The child sought an eidetic-like representation in the auxiliary sign. *In both the Zankov and Yussevich examples, the child reproduced the required word through a process of direct representation rather than mediated symbolization.*

The laws describing the role of sign operations at this stage of development are completely different from the laws describing how the child links up a word with a sign in fully developed sign operations. Children in the experiments just described illustrate a stage of development between the elementary and the completely instrumental process from which fully mediated operations will later develop.

Leontiev's work on the development of sign operations in memory provides examples supporting the theoretical points discussed above as well as later stages in the development of sign operations in memory.[6] He gave a set of twenty words for recall to children of different ages and levels of mental ability. The materials were presented in three ways. First, the words were simply spoken at intervals of about three seconds and the child was told to recall them. In a second task the child was given a set of twenty pictures and told to use them to help recall the words. The pictures were not replicas of the words but were associated with them. In the third series twenty pictures bearing no obvious relation to the to-be-remembered words were used. The basic questions in this research were to what extent can children convert their remembering into a mediated activity using pictures as auxiliary memory aids and how does their success depend upon the different degrees of difficulty represented by the two, potentially mediated, series.

As we might expect, the results differed depending upon the group of children and the difficulty of the recall task. Normal children (ten to twelve years of age) recalled twice as many words when the pictures were available as memory aids as they did without them. They were able to make use of both picture series equally well. Mildly retarded children of the same age benefited little, if at all, from the presence of the pictures; and for severely retarded children, the auxiliary stimuli actually interfered with performance.

The original transcripts from this study clearly show intermediate levels of functioning in which the child attends to the auxiliary picture stimulus and even associates it with the word to be recalled but cannot integrate the stimulus into his system of remembering. Thus, one child selected a picture of an onion to recall the word "dinner." When asked why she chose the picture, she gave the perfectly satisfactory answer, "Because I eat an onion." However, she was unable to recall the word "dinner" during the experiment. This example shows that the ability to form elementary associations is not sufficient to ensure that the associative relation will fulfill the *instrumental* function necessary to produce recall. This kind of evidence leads us to conclude that the development of mediated psychological functions (in this case, mediated memory) represents a special line of development that does not wholly coincide with the development of elementary processes.

I should mention also that the addition of pictures as memory aids did not facilitate recall of adults. The reason for the "failure" is directly opposite to the reasons underlying the failure of memory aids to affect the severely retarded children. In the case of adults, the process of mediated memorizing is so fully developed that it occurs even in the absence of special external aids.

MEMORY AND THINKING

Remembering activities do not simply change as the child grows older; the role of these activities in the system of psychological functions also changes. Nonmediated memory takes place in the context of psychological operations that may have nothing at all in common with the psychological operations that accompany mediated remembering; consequently, experimental results may make it appear that some psychological functions are replaced by others. In other words, with a change in developmental level there occurs a change not so much in the structure of a single function (which, for example, we may call memory) as in the character of those functions with the aid of which remembering takes place; what changes is the *interfunctional* relations that connect memory with other functions.

The memory of older children is not only different from the memory of younger children; it also plays a different role in the older child's cognitive activity. Memory in early childhood is one of the central psychological functions upon which all the other functions are built. Our analyses suggest that thinking in the very young child is in many respects determined by his memory, and is certainly not the same thing as the thinking of the more mature child. For the very young child, to think means to remember; at no time after very early childhood do we see such a close connection between these two psychological functions.

I will give three examples. The first is the definition of concepts in children, which are based on their recollections. If you ask a child to tell you what a snail is, he will say that it is little, it slithers, and it sticks out its foot; if you ask him to tell you what a grandmother is, he is likely to reply, "She has a soft lap." In both cases the child gives a very clear summary of the impressions which the topic has made upon him and which he recollects. The content of the thinking act in the child when defining such concepts is determined not so much by the logical structure of the concept itself as by the child's concrete recollections. It is syncretic in character and reflects the fact that the child's thinking depends first of all on his memory.

Another example is the development of visual concepts in very young children. Investigations of children's thinking when they are required to transpose a relation learned with one set of stimuli to a similar set have shown that their transfer is nothing more than remembering with respect to isolated instances. Their general representations of the world are based on the recall of concrete instances and do not yet possess the character of an abstraction.[7]

The last example concerns the analysis of word meaning. Investigations in this area show that the connections underlying words are fundamentally different in the young child and in the adult. Children's concepts relate to a series of examples and are constructed in a manner similar to the way we represent family names. To name words for them is not so much to indicate familiar concepts as to name familiar families or whole groups of visual things connected by visual ties. In this way the experience of the child and the "unmediated" influence of the child's experience are documented in his memory and directly determine the entire structure of the young child's thought.

All these facts suggest that, from the point of view of psychological development, memory rather than abstract thought is the definitive characteristic of the early stages of cognitive development. However, in the course of development a transformation occurs, especially in adolescence. Investigations of memory at this age have shown that toward the end of childhood the interfunctional relations involving memory reverse their direction. *For the young child, to think means to recall; but for the adolescent, to recall means to think.* Her memory is so "logicalized" that remembering is reduced to establishing and finding logical relations; recognizing consists in discovering that element which the task indicates has to be found.

This logicalization is indicative of how relations among cognitive functions change in the course of development. At the transitional age all ideas and concepts, all mental structures, cease to be organized according to family types and become organized as abstract concepts.

There can be no doubt that to remember an item when thinking in concepts is a completely different task from thinking in complexes, although the processes are compatible with each other.[8] Therefore, the development of children's memory must be studied not only with respect to changes happening within memory itself, but also with respect to the relation between memory and other functions.

When a human being ties a knot in her handkerchief as a reminder, she is, in essence, constructing the process of memorizing by forcing an external object to remind her of something; she transforms remembering into an external activity. This fact alone is enough to demonstrate the fundamental characteristic of the higher forms of behavior. In the elementary form something is remembered; in the higher form humans remember something. In the first case a temporary link is formed owing to the simultaneous occurrence of two stimuli that affect the organism; in the second case humans personally create a temporary link through an artificial combination of stimuli.

The very essence of human memory consists in the fact that human beings actively remember with the help of signs. It may be said that the basic characteristic of human behavior in general is that humans personally influence their relations with the environment and through that environment personally change their behavior, subjugating it to their control. It has been remarked that the very essence of civilization consists of purposely building monuments so as not to forget. In both the knot and the monument we have manifestations of the most fundamental and characteristic feature distinguishing human from animal memory.

4

Internalization of Higher Psychological Functions

When comparing the principles regulating unconditioned and conditioned reflexes, Pavlov uses the example of a telephone call. One possibility is for the call to connect two points directly via a special line. This corresponds to an unconditioned reflex. The other possibility is for the phone call to be relayed through a special, central station with the help of temporary and limitlessly variable connections. This corresponds to a conditioned reflex. The cerebral cortex, as the organ that closes the conditioned reflex circuit, plays the role of such a central station.

The fundamental message of our analysis of the processes that underlie the creation of signs (signalization) may be expressed by a more generalized form of the same metaphor. Let us take the case of tying a knot as a reminder or drawing lots as a means of decision making. There is no doubt that in both cases a temporary conditioned connection is formed, that is, a connection of Pavlov's second type. But if we wish to grasp the essentials of what is happening here, we are forced to take into consideration not only the function of the telephone mechanism but also of the operator who plugged in and thus connected the line. In our example, the connection was established by the person who tied the knot. This feature distinguishes the higher forms of behavior from the lower.

The invention and use of signs as auxiliary means of solving a given psychological problem (to remember, compare something, report, choose, and so on) is analogous to the invention and use of tools in one psychological respect. The sign acts as an instrument of psychological activity in a manner analogous to the role of a tool in labor. But this analogy, like any other, does not imply the identity of these similar concepts. We should not expect to find *many* similarities with tools in those means of adaptation we call signs. What's more, in addition to the similar and common feature shared by the two kinds of activity, we see very essential differences.

Here we want to be as precise as possible. Leaning for support on the term's figurative meaning, some psychologists have used the word "tool" when referring to the indirect function of an object as the means for accomplishing some activity. Expressions such as "the tongue is the tool of thought" or "aides de memoire" are usually bereft of any definite content and hardly mean more than what they really are: simple metaphors and more colorful ways of expressing the fact that certain objects or operations play an auxiliary role in psychological activity.

On the other hand, there have been many attempts to invest such expressions with a literal meaning, to equate the sign with the tool. By erasing the fundamental distinction between them, this approach loses the specific characteristics of each type of activity and leaves us with one general psychological form of determination. This is the position adopted by Dewey, one of pragmatism's representatives. He defines the tongue as the tool of tools, transposing Aristotle's definition of the human hand to speech.

I wish it to be clear that the analogy between sign and tool that I propose is different from either of the approaches just discussed. The uncertain, indistinct meaning that is usually read into the figurative use of the word "tool" in no way eases the researcher's task. His task is to uncover the real relationship, not the figurative one, that exists between behavior and its auxiliary means. Should we conceive of thought or memory as being analogous to external activity? Do the "means of activity" simply play the indefinite role of supporting the psychological process that leans on them? What is the nature of this support? What in general does it mean to be a "means" of thought or of memory? Psychologists who so enjoy using these fuzzy expressions furnish us with no answer to these questions.

But the position of those psychologists who treat such expressions literally turns out to be even fuzzier. Concepts that have a psychological aspect but do not actually belong to psychology—such as "technique"— are psychologized without any grounds whatsoever. Equating psychological and nonpsychological phenomena is possible only if one ignores the essence of each form of activity, as well as the differences between their historic roles and nature. Distinctions between tools as a means of labor, of mastering nature, and language as a means of social intercourse become dissolved in the general concept of artifacts or artificial adaptations.

We seek to understand the behavioral role of the sign in all its uniqueness. This goal has motivated our empirical studies of how both tool and sign use are mutually linked and yet separate in the child's cultural development. We have adopted three conditions as a starting point for this work. The first pertains to the analogy and common points of the two types of activity, the second clarifies their basic differences, and the third attempts to demonstrate the real psychological link existing between the one and the other, or at least to hint at its existence.

As we have already noted, the basic analogy between sign and tool rests on the mediating function that characterizes each of them. They may, therefore, from the psychological perspective, be subsumed under the same category. We can express the logical relationship between the use of signs and of tools using the schema in figure 4, which shows each concept subsumed under the more general concept of indirect (mediated) activity.

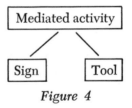

Figure 4

That concept, quite justly, was invested with the broadest general meaning by Hegel, who saw in it a characteristic feature of human reason: "Reason," he wrote, "is just as cunning as she is powerful. Her cunning consists principally in her mediating activity which, by causing objects to act and react on each other in accordance with their own nature, in this way, without any direct interference in the process, carries out reasons' intentions."[1] Marx cites that definition when speaking of working tools, to show that man "uses the mechanical, physical, and chemical properties of objects so as to make them act as forces that affect other objects in order to fulfill his personal goals."[2]

This analysis provides a sound basis for assigning the use of signs to the category of mediated activity, for the essence of sign use consists in man's affecting behavior through signs. In both cases the indirect (mediated) function comes to the forefront. I shall not define further the relation of these jointly subsumed concepts to each other, or their relation to the more generic concept of mediated activity. I should only like to note that neither can, under any circumstance, be considered iso-morphic with respect to the functions they perform, nor can they be seen as *fully* exhausting the concept of mediated activity. A host of other mediated activities might be named; cognitive activity is not limited to the use of tools or signs.

On the purely logical plane of the relation between the two con-cepts, our schema represents the two means of adaptation as diverging lines of mediated activity. This divergence is the basis for our second point. A most essential difference between sign and tool, and the basis for the real divergence of the two lines, is the different ways that they orient human behavior. The tool's function is to serve as the conductor of human influence on the object of activity; it is *externally* oriented; it must lead to changes in objects. It is a means by which human external activity is aimed at mastering, and triumphing over, nature. The sign, on the other hand, changes nothing in the object of a psychological opera-tion. It is a means of internal activity aimed at mastering oneself; the sign is *internally* oriented. These activities are so different from each other that the nature of the means they use cannot be the same in both cases.

Finally, the third point pertains to the real tie between these activi-ties and, hence, to the real tie of their development in phylo- and onto-genesis. The mastering of nature and the mastering of behavior are mutually linked, just as man's alteration of nature alters man's own nature. In phylogenesis we can reconstruct this link through fragmentary but convincing documentary evidence, while in ontogenesis we can trace it experimentally.

One thing is already certain. Just as the first use of tools refutes the notion that development represents the mere unfolding of the child's organically predetermined system of activity, so the first use of signs demonstrates that there cannot be a single organically predetermined internal system of activity that exists for each psychological function. The use of artificial means, the transition to mediated activity, funda-mentally changes all psychological operations just as the use of tools limitlessly broadens the range of activities within which the new psychological functions may operate. In this context, we can use the term *higher* psychological function, or *higher behavior* as referring to the combination of tool and sign in psychological activity.

Several phases in the use of sign operations have been described thus far. In the initial phase reliance upon external signs is crucial to the child's effort. But through development these operations undergo radi-cal changes: the entire operation of mediated activity (for example, memorizing) begins to take place as a purely internal process. Paradoxically, late stages of the child's behavior appear to be the same as early stages of memorizing, which were characterized by a direct process. The very young child does not rely upon external means; rather he uses a "natural," "eidetic" approach. Judging only from external appearances, it seems that the older child has simply begun to memorize more and better; that she has somehow perfected and developed her old methods of memorizing. At the highest levels she appears to have abandoned any reliance upon signs. However, this appearance is only illusory. Development, as often happens, proceeds here not in a circle but in a spiral, passing through the same point at each new revolution while advancing to a higher level.

We call the internal reconstruction of an external operation *internalization*. A good example of this process may be found in the development of pointing. Initially, this gesture is nothing more than an unsuccessful attempt to grasp something, a movement aimed at a certain object which designates forthcoming activity. The child attempts to grasp an object placed beyond his reach; his hands, stretched toward that object, remain poised in the air. His fingers make grasping movements. At this initial stage pointing is represented by the child's movement, which seems to be pointing to an object—that and nothing more.

When the mother comes to the child's aid and realizes his movement indicates something, the situation changes fundamentally. Pointing becomes a gesture for others. The child's unsuccessful attempt engenders a reaction not from the object he seeks but *from another person.* Consequently, the primary meaning of that unsuccessful grasping movement is established by others. Only later, when the child can link his unsuccessful grasping movement to the objective situation as a whole, does he begin to understand this movement as pointing. At this juncture there occurs a change in that movement's function: from an object-oriented movement it becomes a movement aimed at another person, a means of establishing relations. *The grasping movement changes to the act of pointing.* As a result of this change, the movement itself is then physically simplified, and what results is the form of pointing that we may call a true gesture. It becomes a true gesture only after it objectively manifests all the functions of pointing for others and is understood by others as such a gesture. Its meaning and functions are created at first by an objective situation and then by people who surround the child.

As the above description of pointing illustrates, the process of internalization consists of a series of transformations:

(a) *An operation that initially represents an external activity is reconstructed and begins to occur internally*. Of particular importance to the development of higher mental processes is the transformation of sign-using activity, the history and characteristics of which are illustrated by the development of practical intelligence, voluntary attention, and memory.

(b) *An interpersonal process is transformed into an intrapersonal one*. Every function in the child's cultural development appears twice: first, on the social level, and later, on the individual level; first, *between* people (*interpsychological*), and then *inside* the child (*intrapsychological*). This applies equally to voluntary attention, to logical memory, and to the formation of concepts. All the higher functions originate as actual relations between human individuals.

(c) *The transformation of an interpersonal process into an intrapersonal one is the result of a long series of developmental events*. The process being transformed continues to exist and to change as an external form of activity for a long time before definitively turning inward. For many functions, the stage of external signs lasts forever, that is, it is their final stage of development. Other functions develop further and gradually become inner functions. However, they take on the character of inner processes only as a result of a prolonged development. Their transfer inward is linked with changes in the laws governing their activity; they are incorporated into a new system with its own laws.

The internalization of cultural forms of behavior involves the reconstruction of psychological activity on the basis of sign operations. Psychological processes as they appear in animals actually cease to exist; they are incorporated into this system of behavior and are culturally reconstituted and developed to form a new psychological entity. The use of external signs is also radically reconstructed. The developmental changes in sign operations are akin to those that occur in language. Aspects of external or communicative speech as well as egocentric speech turn "inward" to become the basis of inner speech.

The internalization of socially rooted and historically developed activities is the distinguishing feature of human psychology, the basis of the qualitative leap from animal to human psychology. As yet, the barest outline of this process is known.

5

Problems of Method

In general, any fundamentally new approach to a scientific problem inevitably leads to new methods of investigation and analysis. The invention of new methods that are adequate to the new ways in which problems are posed requires far more than a simple modification of previously accepted methods. Contemporary psychological experimentation is no exception in this respect; its methods have always reflected the ways in which fundamental psychological problems were viewed and solved. Therefore, our criticism of current views concerning the essential nature and development of psychological processes must inevitably result in a reexamination of methods of research.

Despite great diversity in procedural details, virtually all psychological experiments rely on what we shall term a stimulus-response *framework*. By this we mean that no matter what psychological process is under discussion, the psychologist seeks to confront the subject with some kind of stimulus situation designed to influence him in a particular way, and then the psychologist examines and analyzes the response(s) elicited by that stimulating situation. After all, the very essence of experimentation is to evoke the phenomenon under study in an artificial (and thereby controllable) way and to study the variations in response that occur in conjunction with various changes in the stimulus.

On the surface it may appear that various schools of psychology could not possibly agree on this methodology. The objective psychology of Watson, Bekhterev, and others, for example, was constructed in opposition to the subjective theories of Wundt and the Würzburg school. But closer examination of the differences between schools of psychology reveals that those differences arise out of the *theoretical interpretation* psychologists want to assign to the consequences of various stimulating environments and not out of variations in the general methodological approach within which observations are made.

Reliance on a stimulus-response framework is an obvious feature of those schools of psychology whose theories as well as experiments are based on stimulus-response interpretations of behavior. Pavlovian theory, for example, has utilized the notion of cortical excitation incited by various stimuli to explain how connections are formed in the brain that enable the organism to learn to respond to hitherto neutral stimuli. It may be less obvious that exactly the same framework applies to introspective psychology as well, since the framework and the theory do not seem to coincide. However, taking Wundt as an example, we find that the stimulus-response framework provided the context within which the experimenter-theorist could obtain descriptions of the processes presumed to have been elicited by the stimulus.

The adoption of a stimulus-response framework by introspective psychology in the 1880s was a revolutionary step forward for psychology because it brought psychology closer to the method and spirit of the natural sciences and prepared the way for the objective psychological approaches that followed. But to claim that both introspective and objective psychology share a common methodological framework does not in any way imply that there are no important differences between them. I am emphasizing their common methodological framework because its recognition helps us to appreciate the fact that introspective psychology was rooted in the firm soil of natural sciences and that psychological processes have long been understood within a reactive context.

It is also important to realize that the experimental method was first formulated by introspective psychologists in that area of psychophysics and psychophysiology that dealt with the simplest psychological phenomena, phenomena that could plausibly be interpreted as directly and uniquely linked to external agents. Wundt, for example, saw the very essence of psychological method as the systematic alteration of the stimuli that generate a change in the psychological process linked to them. He sought the maximally objective way to record the external manifestations of these internal processes, which is what he believed the subject's introspective reports to be.

At the same time, it is important to keep in mind that for Wundt the stimulus and response functioned only to set up the framework within which the important events, psychological processes, could be studied in a reliable and controlled way. Introspective reports of these processes remained the paramount evidence concerning their nature—an interpretation not shared by later investigators.

Our description of the basic framework of psychological experimentation as practiced by Wundt implies limitations on its application: such experimentation was considered adequate only to the study of elementary processes of a psychophysiological character. The higher psychological functions did not allow study in this form and thus remained a closed book as far as experimental psychology was concerned. If we recall the kinds of experimentation on the cognitive development of children that characterized the research reviewed in earlier chapters of this book, we can easily understand why previous investigators concentrated on elementary psychological functions; this limitation is a built-in feature of the experimental method as it was generally accepted in psychology. Wundt understood and accepted this fact, which is why he eschewed *experimental* studies of higher psychological functions.

From the foregoing it should be clear that a stimulus-response framework for constructing experimental observations *cannot* serve as the basis for the adequate study of the higher, specifically human forms of behavior. At best it can only help us to record the existence of the lower, subordinated forms, which do not capture the essence of the higher forms. Using current methods, we can only determine quantitative variation in the complexity of stimuli and in the responses of different animals and humans at different stages of development.

It is my belief, based upon a dialectical materialist approach to the analysis of human history, that human behavior differs qualitatively from animal behavior to the same extent that the adaptability and historical development of humans differ from the adaptability and development of animals. The psychological development of humans is part of the general historical development of our species and must be so understood. Acceptance of this proposition means that we must find a new methodology for psychological experimentation.

The keystone of our method, which I will try to describe analytically in the following sections, follows directly from the contrast Engels drew between naturalistic and dialectical approaches to the understanding of human history. Naturalism in historical analysis, according to Engels, manifests itself in the assumption that only nature affects human beings and only natural conditions determine historical development. The dialectical approach, while admitting the influence of nature on man, asserts that man, in turn, affects nature and creates through his changes in nature new natural conditions for his existence.[1] This position is the keystone of our approach to the study and interpretation of man's higher psychological functions and serves as the basis for the new methods of experimentation and analysis that we advocate.

All stimulus-response methods share the inadequacy that Engels ascribes to naturalistic approaches to history. Both see the relation between human behavior and nature as unidirectionally reactive. My collaborators and I, however, believe that human behavior comes to have that "transforming reaction on nature" which Engels attributed to tools. We must, then, seek methods adequate to our conception. In conjunction with new methods, we also need a new analytic framework.

I have emphasized that a basic goal of our research is to provide an analysis of the higher forms of behavior, but the situation in contemporary psychology is such that the problem of analysis itself must be discussed if our approach is to be generalized beyond the specific examples presented.

Three principles form the basis of our approach to the analysis of higher psychological functions.

Analyzing process, not objects. The first principle leads us to distinguish between the analysis of an object and of a process. As Koffka put it, psychological analysis has almost always treated the processes it analyzes as stable, fixed objects. The task of analysis consisted in breaking these forms down into their components. Psychological analysis of objects should be contrasted with the analysis of processes, which requires a dynamic display of the main points making up the processes' history. Consequently, developmental psychology, not experimental psychology, provides the new approach to analysis that we need. Like Werner, we are advocating the developmental approach as an essential addition to experimental psychology.[2] Any psychological process, whether the development of thought or voluntary behavior, is a process undergoing changes right before one's eyes. The development in question can be limited to only a few seconds, or even fractions of seconds (as is the case in normal perception). It can also (as in the case of complex mental processes) last many days and even weeks. Under certain conditions it becomes possible to trace this development. Werner's work furnishes one example of how a developmental viewpoint may be applied to experimental research. Using such an approach, one can, under laboratory conditions, provoke development.

Our method may be called experimental-developmental in the sense that it artificially provokes or creates a process of psychological development. This approach is equally appropriate to the basic aim of dynamic analysis. If we replace object analysis by process analysis, then the basic task of research obviously becomes a reconstruction of each stage in the development of the process: the process must be turned back to its initial stages.

Explanation versus description. In associationistic and introspective psychology, analysis is essentially description and not explanation as we understand it. Mere description does not reveal the actual causal-dynamic relations that underlie phenomena.

K. Lewin contrasts phenomenological analysis, which is based on external features (phenotypes), with what he calls genotypic analysis, wherein a phenomenon is explained on the basis of its origin rather than its outer appearance.[3] The difference between these two points of view can be elucidated by any biological example. A whale, from the point of view of its outer appearance, stands closer to the fish family than to the mammal, but in its biological nature it is closer to a cow or a deer than to a pike or a shark. Following Lewin, we can apply this distinction between the phenotypic (descriptive) and genotypic (explanatory) viewpoints to psychology. By a developmental study of a problem, I mean the disclosure of its genesis, its causal dynamic basis. By pheno-typic I mean the analysis that begins directly with an object's current features and manifestations. It is possible to furnish many examples from psychology where serious errors have been committed because these viewpoints have been confused. In our study of the development of speech, we have emphasized the importance of the distinction between phenotypic and genotypic similarities.

In their external, descriptive aspects, the first manifestation of speech in the one-and-a-half to two-year-old child are similar to adult speech. On the basis of this similarity, such serious researchers as Stern come to the conclusion that in essence the eighteen-month-old child is already conscious of the relation between sign and meaning.[4] In other words, he classes together phenomena that have absolutely nothing in common from the developmental point of view. On the other hand, ego-centric speech—which in its outer manifestations differs from internal speech in essential ways—must be classed together with internal speech from the developmental point of view.

Our research on young children's speech brings us to the basic principle formulated by Lewin: two phenotypically identical or similar processes may be radically different from each other in their causal-dynamic aspects and vice versa; two processes that are very close in their causal-dynamic nature may be very different phenotypically.

I have said that the phenotypic approach categorizes processes according to their external similarities. Marx commented on the phenotypic approach in a most general form when he stated that "if the essence of objects coincided with the form of their outer manifestations, then every science would be superfluous"—an extremely reasonable observation.[5] If every object was phenotypically and genotypically equivalent (that is, if the true principles of its construction and operation were expressed by its outer manifestation), then everyday experience would fully suffice to replace scientific analysis. Everything we saw would be the subject of our scientific knowledge.

In reality, psychology teaches us at every step that though two types of activity can have the same external manifestation, whether in origin or essence, their nature may differ most profoundly. In such cases special means of scientific analysis are necessary in order to lay bare internal differences that are hidden by external similarities. It is the task of analysis to reveal these relations. In that sense, real scientific analysis differs radically from subjective, introspective analysis, which by its very nature cannot hope to go beyond pure description. The kind of objective analysis we advocate seeks to lay bare the essence rather than the perceived characteristics of psychological phenomena.

For example, we are not interested in a description of the immediate experience elicited by a flashing light as it is revealed to us by introspective analysis; rather we seek to understand the real links between the external stimuli and internal responses that underlie the higher form of behavior named by introspective descriptions. Thus, psychological analysis in our sense rejects nominal descriptions and seeks instead to determine causal-dynamic relations. However, such explanation would also be impossible if we ignored the external manifestations of things. By necessity, objective analysis includes a scientific explanation of both external manifestations and the process under study. Analysis is not limited to a developmental perspective. It does not repudiate the explanation of current phenotypical idiosyncrasies, but rather subordinates them to the discovery of their actual origin.

The problem of "fossilized behavior." The third principle underlying our analytic approach is based on the fact that in psychology we often meet with processes that have already died away, that is, processes that have gone through a very long stage of historical development and have become fossilized. These fossilized forms of behavior are most easily found in the so-called automated or mechanized psychological processes which, owing to their ancient origins, are now being repeated for the millionth time and have become mechanized. They have lost their original appearance, and their outer appearance tells us nothing whatsoever about their internal nature. Their automatic character creates great difficulties for psychological analysis.

The processes that have traditionally been referred to as voluntary and involuntary attention provide an elementary example that demonstrates how essentially different processes acquire outer similarity as a result of this automation. Developmentally speaking, these two processes differ very profoundly. But in experimental psychology it is considered a fact, as formulated by Titchener, that voluntary attention, once established, functions just like involuntary attention.[6] In Titchener's terms, "secondary" attention constantly changes into "primary" attention. Having described and contrasted the two types of attention, Titchener then says, "There exists, however, a third stage in the development of attention, and it consists in nothing less than a return to the first stage." The last and highest stage in the development of any process may demonstrate a purely phenotypic similarity with the first or primary stages, and if we take a phenotypic approach, it is impossible to distinguish between higher and lower forms of this process. The only way to study this third and highest stage in the development of attention is to understand it in all its idiosyncrasies and differences. In short, we need to understand its origin. It follows, then, that we need to concentrate not on the *product* of development but on the very *process* by which higher forms are established. To do so the researcher is often forced to alter the automatic, mechanized, fossilized character of the higher form of behavior and to turn it back to its source through the experiment. This is the aim of dynamic analysis.

Inactive, rudimentary functions stand not as the living remnants of biological evolution but as those of the historical development of behavior. Consequently, the study of rudimentary functions must be the point of departure for evolving a historical perspective in psychological experiments. It is here that the past and the present are fused and the present is seen in the light of history. Here we find ourselves simultaneously on two planes: that which is and that which was. The fossilized form is the end of the thread that ties the present to the past, the higher stages of development to the primary ones.

The concept of a historically based psychology is misunderstood by most researchers who study child development. For them, to study something historically means, by definition, to study some past event. Hence, they naively imagine an insurmountable barrier between historic study and study of present-day behavioral forms. *To study some-*

thing historically means to study it in the process of change; that is the dialectical method's basic demand. To encompass in research the process of a given thing's development in all its phases and changes—from birth to death—fundamentally means to discover its nature, its essence, for "it is only in movement that a body shows what it is." Thus, the historical study of behavior is not an auxiliary aspect of theoretical study, but rather forms its very base. As P. P. Blonsky has stated, "Behavior can be understood only as the history of behavior."[7]

The search for method becomes one of the most important problems of the entire enterprise of understanding the uniquely human forms of psychological activity. In this case, the method is simultaneously prerequisite and product, the tool and the result of the study.

In summary, then, the aim of psychological analysis and its essential factors are as follows: (1) process analysis as opposed to object analysis; (2) analysis that reveals real, causal or dynamic relations as opposed to enumeration of a process's outer features, that is, explanatory, not descriptive, analysis; and (3) developmental analysis that returns to the source and reconstructs all the points in the development of a given structure. The result of development will be neither a purely psychological structure such as descriptive psychology considers the result to be, nor a simple sum of elementary processes such as associationistic psychology saw it, but a qualitatively new form that appears in the process of development.

THE PSYCHOLOGY OF COMPLEX CHOICE RESPONSES

In order to illustrate the contrasting approaches to psychological analysis, I will discuss in some detail two different analyses of one task. In the task I have chosen, the subject is presented one or more stimuli (visually or auditorily as a rule). The required response differs according to the number of stimuli and the interests of the investigator: some approaches seek to break the reaction down into a series of elementary processes whose durations can be added and subtracted to establish the laws of their combination; others seek to describe the emotional reaction of the subject as he responds to the stimulus. In either case, the subjects' introspective analyses of their responses are used as basic data. In these experiments the inadequacies of prior formulations provide useful illustrations of our basic analytic principles.[8]

It is also characteristic of these analyses that complex and simple responses are distinguished primarily by the quantitative complexity of the stimuli: a simple reaction is said to occur when a single stimulus is presented, and the complexity of the response is said to increase with an increasing number of stimuli. An essential presumption in this line of thinking is that the complexity of the task is identical to the complexity of the subject's internal response.

This identity is clearly expressed in the algebraic formulas commonly used in the analysis of responses to such tasks. If we present a single stimulus, we can write an equation in which the complex reaction is equivalent to a simple reaction (sensory recognition): $R_t = R_s$ where R_t is the response time for the total, complex reaction and R_s is the response time for a single recognition reaction. If we present two or more stimuli, from which the subject must select one, this equation becomes: $R_t = R_s + D$, where D is the time taken to discriminate between the target stimulus and the remainder. Using these two equations, we could establish the time required both for a simple reaction and for the discriminative reaction. If we complicate the task by requiring the subject to choose a different response for each stimulus (for example, press the left-hand key for stimulus A and the right-hand key for stimulus B), we obtain the classical choice reaction formula: $R_t = R_s + D + C$, where C is the time required to choose the correct movement, for example, to press the key corresponding to the stimulus presented.

A verbal description of the theory underlying this set of formulas would be the following: the discrimination response is a simple reaction plus discrimination; the choice reaction is a simple reaction plus discrimination plus choice. The higher, more complex response is seen as the arithmetic sum of its elementary components.

Proponents of this analytic approach apply it quite widely. Thus, for example, Cattell believes that by subtracting the time needed to comprehend and name a word from the time needed to comprehend, translate a word into another language, and name it, we can obtain a pure measure of the translation process.[9] In short, even higher processes such as speech comprehension and production can be analyzed by these methods. A more mechanical notion of the complex, higher forms of behavior would be hard to imagine.

However, this analytic approach has been shown to lead to a variety of difficulties. The most basic, empirical observation that contradicts this theory comes from Titchener, who pointed out that the time to execute a carefully prepared choice reaction may be equal to the reaction time for a simple, sensory response. By the logic of the analysis summarized in the equations given above, this state of affairs is impossible.

In our view, the basic premise underlying this entire line of analysis is incorrect. It is not true that a complex reaction consists of a chain of separate processes which may be arbitrarily added and subtracted. Any such reaction reflects processes that depend upon the entire process of learning at every level of practice. This mechanical analysis substitutes relations existing between stimuli for the real relations underlying the process of choosing. This kind of substitution reflects a general intellectualism in psychology which seeks to understand psychological processes in the manipulations that make up the experiment itself; experimental procedures become surrogates for psychological processes.

While various scholars have demonstrated the inadequacy of psychological analysis based upon a mechanical decomposition of responses into their elements, these critics face the problem that their introspective analyses of complex reactions must be restricted to description: the description of external responses is replaced by the description of internal feelings. In either case, we are restricted to phenotypical psychological analysis.

Introspective analysis in which highly trained observers are instructed to note every aspect of their own conscious experience cannot carry us very far. A curious result of this work, as Ach put it in discussing choice reaction studies, has been the discovery that there are no conscious feelings of choice in the choice reaction.[10] Titchener emphasized that one must keep in mind the fact that the names given to a complex or simple reaction (for example, "differentiation" or "choice") refer to the external conditions of the task. We do not differentiate in the differentiation reaction and we do not choose in the choice reaction.

This kind of analysis broke the identity between experimental procedures and psychological processes. Process names like "choosing" and "differentiating" were treated as leftovers from a previous era of psychology when experimentation was still unknown: introspective observers were trained to make a clear distinction between process names and their conscious experience in order to circumvent this problem.

These introspective studies resulted in the conclusion that a situation which seems to require choice processes furnishes no grounds for speaking of a psychological choice response; talk of such responses was replaced by a description of the subjects' feelings during the experiment. But no one could provide evidence that these feelings were an integral part of the particular response process. It seems more likely that they are only one of its components, and require explanation themselves; we are led to conclude that introspection is often unable to provide an accurate description, let alone a correct explanation, for even the subjective aspect of the response. For the same reasons, the frequent discrepancies among the introspective descriptions of various observers which plague this area of research might be expected. It should be clear that introspective analysis cannot provide a real causal or dynamic explanation of a process; for that to occur, we must give up reliance on phenotypic appearances and move to a developmental viewpoint.

Research on complex reactions also illustrates psychology's reliance on the analysis of processes only after they have become fossilized. This point was noted by Titchener, who remarked that researchers have concentrated on the reaction time of the responses they study, not on the learning processes or the content of the reaction itself. This same conclusion is seen clearly in the standard practice of discarding the data from early sessions when the response is being established. Uniformity was sought, so that it was never possible to grasp the process in flight; instead, researchers routinely discarded the critical time when a reaction appears and when its functional links are established and adjusted. Such practices lead us to characterize the responses as "fossilized." They reflect the fact that these psychologists were not interested in complex reactions as a process of development. This approach is also a major cause of the confusions which arose concerning complex and simple reactions that have surface similarities. It might be said that complex reactions have been studied postmortem.

Another perspective on this issue can be gained from comparing complex reactions with reflexes, which are psychologically different in many respects. One point of comparison will suffice for purposes of illustration. It is well known that the latent period for a complex reaction is longer than the latent period for a reflex. But Wundt long ago established that the latent period of a complex reaction decreases with practice. As a result, the latency of the complex reaction and the simple reflex become equivalent. The most important differences between a complex reaction and a reflex are usually most apparent when the reaction is in its early stages; as practice proceeds, the differences become more and more obscured. Therefore, the differences between these two forms of behavior should be sought in the analysis of their development. But instead of increasing the discernible differences between them, investigations of well-practiced choice reactions and reflexes hide these differences. The preparatory trials demanded by standard experimental methods often last for several long sessions. When these data are then discarded or ignored, the researcher is left with an automatized reaction that has lost its developmental difference from a reflex and has acquired a surface, phenotypical similarity to it. These factors have led to our assertion that previous researchers have studied reactions in psychological experiments only after they have become fossilized.

This discussion of traditional analyses of complex reaction defines, albeit negatively, the basic tasks confronting us. In order to obtain the kind of causal-dynamic analysis we have been advocating, we will have to shift the focus of our research.

A CAUSAL–DYNAMIC STUDY OF CHOICE REACTIONS

Obviously, the early sessions during which a reaction is formed are of crucial concern because only data from this period will reveal the reaction's true origin and its links to other processes. Through an objective study of the entire history of the reaction, we can obtain an integrated explanation of both its internal and surface manifestations. Thus, we will want to study the reaction as it appears initially, as it takes shape, and after it is firmly formed, constantly keeping in mind the dynamic flow of the entire process of its development.

From my previous discussion, another part of the task is clear: the complex reaction must be studied as a living process, not as an object. We must transform the reaction back to its source if we encounter it in automatized form.

When we examine the experimental procedures used in complex reactions, we find that all are restricted to meaningless connections between stimuli and responses. The subject is presented several stimuli to which he must respond in different ways: neither the relations between the stimuli and the required responses nor the sequence in which the stimuli are presented have any significance from the subject's point of view. When a motor response, such as a key press, is required, subjects may make the movement in any way they like. These conventions render the relations among the elements of the problem mechanical in principle and place the procedures on a plane with the research on memory that uses nonsense stimuli.

This analogy between choice reaction and memory studies can be extended by considering the similarity of the role of repetition in the two tasks. Although no one has dwelt on a study of the practice trials in choice reaction studies, it is safe to conclude that if the reaction is formed through repeated training (or training plus written or oral instruction), it has been learned by rote, just as learning the connection between two nonsense syllables is a rote process. If simple reactions were involved and the subject was given extensive explanation ahead of time so that the relation between stimulus and response were meaningful (for example, push key number 1 when I say "one," push key number 2 when I say "two"), we would be dealing with already existing links. In neither case could we study the process of organizing the reaction, during which its underlying links would be discoverable.

To make all of this clear, let us trace the stages through which the choice reaction moves, first in experiments with adults and then with children.

If we set up a relatively simple choice reaction, say, pressing a button with the left hand when a red stimulus is shown and pressing with the right hand when a green stimulus is shown, adults quickly acquire a stable response. Suppose, however, we increase the number of stimuli and responses to five or six and diversify the responses so that the subject has to respond not only with both hands, but sometimes pressing a button and sometimes simply by moving a finger. With this larger number of stimulus-response pairings, the task is considerably more difficult. Suppose further that instead of a lengthy pretraining period in which the subject is allowed to learn the stimulus-response relations, we give only minimal instructions. Faced with this situation, adults often refused even to attempt to deal with the problem, objecting that they could not remember what to do. Even after the session started, they kept repeating the instructions to themselves, asked about aspects of the task they had forgotten, and generally sought to master the entire system of relations as a whole before they settled down to the task as it is usually conceived.

However, if we placed additional stimuli on the response buttons and keys in a manner analogous to the procedures in previously described memory studies, the adults immediately used these auxiliary means to remember the necessary stimulus-response relations.

Among young children, a different picture emerged. We first presented the problem as we did with adults, by asking the child to make a number of different responses to different stimuli. Unlike the adults, children six to eight years of age often started right into the task after listening to the instructions and attempted to follow them without the slightest hesitation. As soon as the experiment began, most children found themselves in great difficulty. If a child recalled one or two of the required relations and responded correctly to those stimuli, he would naively ask about the remaining stimuli, treating each of them in isolation from each other. This behavior contrasted with that of the adults who generally failed to deal effectively with the individual stimuli until all the necessary relations were mastered. We view this behavior on the part of the children as evidence that they are in the stage of responding to the task in a natural or primitive manner because they rely on unmediated memory for the task elements. The fact that children would unhesitatingly accept the challenge of establishing a complex choice response to as many as ten stimuli suggests that they do not yet know their own capacities and limitations. They operate with complex tasks in the same way they operate with simple ones.

The child's behavior also differs from adult behavior when we introduce auxiliary stimuli, although we can discern the beginnings of the restructuring that characterize the adult.

First, we introduce auxiliary stimuli that bear a clear relation to the primary stimuli with which we began. For example, if the primary stimulus was a horse, in response to which the child was supposed to press a key with his left index finger, we pasted a picture of a sleigh on that key. On the key corresponding to a loaf of bread we pasted a picture of a knife. In this case, the child understands that sleigh goes with horse, the knife with bread, and so on. Choice reactions are smoothly established from the outset. Furthermore, it does not matter how many stimuli and responses are involved; the qualitative features of responding remain the same. The child quickly works out a rule for the problem's solution and makes his choice on the basis of this rule.

It would be incorrect, however, to assume that the child has mastered a mediated system of behavior in its full, adult form. We need only to change the relations among the primary and auxiliary stimuli to discover the limits of the child's response system. If we pair the stimuli in a different way (say, horse with knife, bread with sleigh) the child will no longer use the auxiliary stimuli in a proper way. The child recalls only that horse helped to find sleigh in some way. He reveals by his responses that he had been using the conventional association of horse and sleigh to guide the choice, but had not mastered the internal logic of using one stimulus to mediate the response to another.

If we continue our experiment long enough, we will begin to see changes in the way the child responds. In the first stage of responding to arbitrarily related stimuli, the child has insufficient experience with the task to organize his behavior effectively. He uses experience naively. But in the course of the experiment, he gains experience necessary for restructuring his behavior. Just as naive physical knowledge is acquired as the child operates with objects, knowledge of psychological operations is acquired as the child strives to carry out the choice reaction task. As he attempts to recall which stimuli are linked to which responses, the child begins to learn what remembering in this situation consists of and begins to use one or another of the auxiliary stimuli effectively. The child begins to realize that certain relations among the stimuli and auxiliary pictures produce correct choice responses, while others do not. He soon begins to object to the arrangement of pictures, asking that the pictures on the keys be arranged to fit the primary stimuli that are associated with the key. When told to press the bread key in response to the horse picture, the child answers "No, I want the sleigh key." This shows that the child is accumulating experience which is changing the structure of his own memorizing.

Having naively comprehended what the memorizing operations require, the child moves to the following stage. If presented with primary and auxiliary stimuli in an arrangement that seems haphazard, the child will ask to put them in a special order, thus personally establishing a specific relation between them. At this point the child is showing that he knows that certain signs will help to achieve certain operations. In short, he is beginning to memorize through the use of signs.

Once this happens, the child no longer experiences difficulties in creating relations and using them. Given some pairing of primary and auxiliary stimuli, the child is no longer restricted to using already available relations (such as horse–sleigh) but can create relations of his own. This may be called the stage of external sign use. It is characterized by the independent formation of new relations in the child's internal operations using externally presented signs. Now the child is organizing external stimuli to carry out its responses. This fundamental stage is then followed by the stage at which the child begins to organize stimuli of an internal nature.

These changes are manifested in the course of the choice reaction experiment. After considerable practice in the choice experiment, the reaction time begins to grow shorter and shorter. If the reaction time to a particular stimulus had been 500 milliseconds or more, it reduces to a mere 200 milliseconds. The longer reaction time reflected the fact that the child was using external means to carry out the operations of remembering which key to push. Gradually, the child casts off the external stimuli, no longer paying attention to them. The response to the external auxiliary stimuli is replaced by a response to internally produced stimuli. In its most developed form, this internal operation consists of the child grasping the very structure of the process, learning to understand the laws according to which external signs must be used. When this stage is reached, the child will say, "I don't need pictures anymore. I'll do it myself."

CHARACTERISTICS OF THE NEW METHOD

I have attempted to demonstrate that the course of child development is characterized by a radical alteration in the very structure of behavior; at each new stage the child changes not only her response but carries out that response in new ways, drawing on new "instruments" of behavior and replacing one psychological function by another. Psychological operations that were achieved through direct forms of adaptation at early stages are later accomplished through indirect means. The growing complexity of children's behavior is reflected in the changed means they use to fulfill new tasks and the corresponding reconstruction of their psychological processes.

Our concept of development implies a rejection of the frequently held view that cognitive development results from the gradual accumulation of separate changes. We believe that child development is a complex dialectical process characterized by periodicity, unevenness in the development of different functions, metamorphosis or qualitative transformation of one form into another, intertwining of external and internal factors, and adaptive processes which overcome impediments that the child encounters. Steeped in the notion of evolutionary change, most workers in child psychology ignore those turning points, those spasmodic and revolutionary changes that are so frequent in the history of child development. To the naive mind, revolution and evolution seem incompatible and historic development continues only so long as it follows a straight line. Where upheavals occur, where the historical fabric is ruptured, the naive mind sees only catastrophe, gaps, and discontinuity. History seems to stop dead, until it once again takes the direct, linear path of development.

Scientific thought, on the contrary, sees revolution and evolution as two forms of development that are mutually related and mutually presuppose each other. Leaps in the child's development are seen by the scientific mind as no more than a moment in the general line of development.

As I have repeatedly emphasized, an essential mechanism of the reconstructive processes that take place during a child's development is the creation and use of a number of artificial stimuli. These play an auxiliary role that permits human beings to master their own behavior, at first by external means and later by more complex inner operations. Our approach to the study of cognitive functioning does not require the experimenter to furnish subjects with ready-made, external or artificial means in order that they may successfully complete the given task. The experiment is equally valid if, instead of giving children artificial means, the experimenter waits until they spontaneously apply some new auxiliary method or symbol that they then incorporate into their operations.

The specific area to which we apply this approach is not important.

We might study the development of memorizing in children by making available to them new means for solving the given task and then observing the degree and character of their problem-solving efforts. We might use this method to study how children organize their active attention with the aid of external means. We might trace the development of arithmetic skills in young children by making them manipulate objects and apply methods either suggested to them or "invented" by them. What is crucial is that in all these cases we must adhere to one principle. We study *not only the final effect of the operation, but its specific psychological structure.* In all these cases, the psychological structure of the development appears with much greater richness and variety than in the classic method of the simple stimulus-response experiment. Although stimulus-response methodology makes it extremely easy to ascertain subjects' responses, it proves useless when our objective is to discover the means and methods that subjects use to organize their own behavior.

Our approach to the study of these processes is to use what we call *the functional method of double stimulation.* The task facing the child in the experimental context is, as a rule, beyond his present capabilities and cannot be solved by existing skills. In such cases a neutral object is placed near the child, and frequently we are able to observe how the neutral stimulus is drawn into the situation and takes on the function of a sign. Thus, the child actively incorporates these neutral objects into the task of problem solving. We might say that when difficulties arise, neutral stimuli take on the function of a sign and from that point on the operation's structure assumes an essentially different character.

By using this approach, we do not limit ourselves to the usual method of offering the subject simple stimuli to which we expect a direct response. Rather, we simultaneously offer a *second series of stimuli* that have a special function. In this way, we are able to study the *process of accomplishing a task by the aid of specific auxiliary means;* thus we are also able to discover the inner structure and development of the higher psychological processes.

The method of double stimulation elicits manifestations of the crucial processes in the behavior of people of all ages. Tying a knot as a reminder, in both children and adults, is but one example of a pervasive regulatory principle of human behavior, that of *signification,* wherein people create temporary links and give significance to previously neutral stimuli in the context of their problem-solving efforts.

We regard our method as important because it helps to *objectify* inner psychological processes; stimulus-response methods are objective, but they are limited to the study of external responses that are usually in the subject's repertoire to begin with. We believe that our approach to objectifying inner psychological processes is much more adequate, where the goals of psychological research are concerned, than the method of studying preexisting, objective responses.[11] Only the objectification of the inner process guarantees access to specific forms of higher behavior as opposed to subordinate forms.

Part Two / Mind in Society

Educational Implications

6

Interaction between Learning and Development

The problems encountered in the psychological analysis of teaching cannot be correctly resolved or even formulated without addressing the relation between learning and development in school-age children. Yet it is the most unclear of all the basic issues on which the application of child development theories to educational processes depends. Needless to say, the lack of theoretical clarity does not mean that the issue is removed altogether from current research efforts into learning; not one study can avoid this central theoretical issue. But the relation between learning and development remains methodologically unclear because concrete research studies have embodied theoretically vague, critically unevaluated, and sometimes internally contradictory postulates, premises, and peculiar solutions to the problem of this fundamental relationship; and these, of course, result in a variety of errors.

Essentially, all current conceptions of the relation between development and learning in children can be reduced to three major theoretical positions.

The first centers on the assumption that processes of child development are independent of learning. Learning is considered a purely external process that is not actively involved in development. It merely utilizes the achievements of development rather than providing an impetus for modifying its course.

In experimental investigations of the development of thinking in school children, it has been assumed that processes such as deduction and understanding, evolution of notions about the world, interpretation of physical causality, and mastery of logical forms of thought and abstract logic all occur by themselves, without any influence from school learning. An example of such a theory is Piaget's extremely complex and interesting theoretical principles, which also shape the experimental methodology he employs. The questions Piaget uses in the course of his "clinical conversations" with children clearly illustrate his approach. When a five-year-old is asked "why doesn't the sun fall?" it is assumed that the child has neither a ready answer for such a question nor the general capabilities for generating one. The point of asking questions that are so far beyond the reach of the child's intellectual skills is to eliminate the influence of previous experience and knowledge. The experimenter seeks to obtain the tendencies of children's thinking in "pure" form, entirely independent of learning.[1]

Similarly, the classics of psychological literature, such as the works by Binet and others, assume that development is always a prerequisite for learning and that if a child's mental functions (intellectual operations) have not matured to the extent that he is capable of learning a particular subject, then no instruction will prove useful. They especially feared premature instruction, the teaching of a subject before the child was ready for it. All effort was concentrated on finding the lower threshold of learning ability, the age at which a particular kind of learning first becomes possible.

Because this approach is based on the premise that learning trails behind development, that development always outruns learning, it precludes the notion that learning may play a role in the course of the development or maturation of those functions activated in the course of learning. Development or maturation is viewed as a precondition of learning but never the result of it. To summarize this position: Learning forms a superstructure over development, leaving the latter essentially unaltered.

The second major theoretical position is that learning *is* development. This identity is the essence of a group of theories that are quite diverse in origin.

One such theory is based on the concept of reflex, an essentially old notion that has been extensively revived recently. Whether reading, writing, or arithmetic is being considered, development is viewed as the mastery of conditioned reflexes; that is, the process of learning is completely and inseparably blended with the process of development. This notion was elaborated by James, who reduced the learning process to habit formation and identified the learning process with development.

Reflex theories have at least one thing in common with theories such as Piaget's: in both, development is conceived of as the elaboration and substitution of innate responses. As James expressed it, "Education, in short, cannot be better described than by calling it the organization of acquired habits of conduct and tendencies to behavior."[2] Development itself is reduced primarily to the accumulation of all possible responses. Any acquired response is considered either a more complex form of or a substitute for the innate response.

But despite the similarity between the first and second theoretical positions, there is a major difference in their assumptions about the temporal relationship between learning and developmental processes. Theorists who hold the first view assert that developmental cycles precede learning cycles; maturation precedes learning and instruction must lag behind mental growth. For the second group of theorists, both processes occur simultaneously; learning and development coincide at all points in the same way that two identical geometrical figures coincide when superimposed.

The third theoretical position on the relation between learning and development attempts to overcome the extremes of the other two by simply combining them. A clear example of this approach is Koffka's theory, in which development is based on two inherently different but related processes, each of which influences the other.[3] On the one hand is maturation, which depends directly on the development of the nervous system; on the other hand is learning, which itself is also a developmental process.

Three aspects of this theory are new. First, as we already noted, is the combination of two seemingly opposite viewpoints, each of which has been encountered separately in the history of science. The very fact that these two viewpoints can be combined into one theory indicates that they are not opposing and mutually exclusive but have something essential in common. Also new is the idea that the two processes that make up development are mutually dependent and interactive. Of course, the nature of the interaction is left virtually unexplored in Koffka's work, which is limited solely to very general remarks regarding the relation between these two processes. It is clear that for Koffka the process of maturation prepares and makes possible a specific process of learning. The learning process then stimulates and pushes forward the maturation process. The third and most important new aspect of this theory is the expanded role it ascribes to learning in child development. This emphasis leads us directly to an old pedagogical problem, that of formal discipline and the problem of transfer.

Pedagogical movements that have emphasized formal discipline and urged the teaching of classical languages, ancient civilizations, and mathematics have assumed that regardless of the irrelevance of these particular subjects for daily living, they were of the greatest value for the pupil's mental development. A variety of studies have called into question the soundness of this idea. It has been shown that learning in one area has very little influence on overall development. For example, reflex theorists Woodworth and Thorndike found that adults who, after special exercises, had achieved considerable success in determining the length of short lines, had made virtually no progress in their ability to determine the length of long lines. These same adults were successfully trained to estimate the size of a given two-dimensional figure, but this training did not make them successful in estimating the size of a series of other two-dimensional figures of various sizes and shapes.

According to Thorndike, theoreticians in psychology and education believe that every particular response acquisition directly enhances overall ability in equal measure.[4] Teachers believed and acted on the basis of the theory that the mind is a complex of abilities—powers of observation, attention, memory, thinking, and so forth—and that any improvement in any specific ability results in a general improvement in all abilities. According to this theory, if the student increased the attention he paid to Latin grammar, he would increase his abilities to focus attention on any task. The words "accuracy," "quick-wittedness," "ability to reason," "memory," "power of observation," "attention," "concentration," and so forth are said to denote actual fundamental capabilities that vary in accordance with the material with which they operate; these basic abilities are substantially modified by studying particular subjects, and they retain these modifications when they turn to other areas. Therefore, if someone learns to do any single thing well, he will also be able to do other entirely unrelated things well as a result of some secret connection. It is assumed that mental capabilities function independently of the material with which they operate, and that the development of one ability entails the development of others.

Thorndike himself opposed this point of view. Through a variety of studies he showed that particular forms of activity, such as spelling, are dependent on the mastery of specific skills and material necessary for the performance of that particular task. The development of one particular capability seldom means the development of others. Thorndike argued that specialization of abilities is even greater than superficial observation may indicate. For example, if, out of a hundred individuals we choose ten who display the ability to detect spelling errors or to measure lengths, it is unlikely that these ten will display better abilities regarding, for example, the estimation of the weight of objects. In the same way, speed and accuracy in adding numbers are entirely unrelated to speed and accuracy in being able to think up antonyms.

This research shows that the mind is not a complex network of general capabilities such as observation, attention, memory, judgment, and so forth, but a set of specific capabilities, each of which is, to some extent, independent of the others and is developed independently. Learning is more than the acquisition of the ability to think; it is the acquisition of many specialized abilities for thinking about a variety of things. Learning does not alter our overall ability to focus attention but rather develops various abilities to focus attention on a variety of things. According to this view, special training affects overall development only when its elements, material, and processes are similar across specific domains; habit governs us. This leads to the conclusion that because each activity depends on the material with which it operates, the development of consciousness is the development of a set of particular, independent capabilities or of a set of particular habits. Improvement of one function of consciousness or one aspect of its activity can affect the development of another only to the extent that there are elements common to both functions or activities.

Developmental theorists such as Koffka and the Gestalt School—who hold to the third theoretical position outlined earlier—oppose Thorndike's point of view. They assert that the influence of learning is never specific. From their study of structural principles, they argue that the learning process can never be reduced simply to the formation of skills but embodies an intellectual order that makes it possible to transfer general principles discovered in solving one task to a variety of other tasks. From this point of view, the child, while learning a particular operation, acquires the ability to create structures of a certain type, regardless of the diverse materials with which she is working and regardless of the particular elements involved. Thus, Koffka does not conceive of learning as limited to a process of habit and skill acquisition. The relationship he posits between learning and development is not that of an identity but of a more complex relationship. According to Thorndike, learning and development coincide at all points, but for Koffka, development is always a larger set than learning. Schematically, the relationship between the two processes could be depicted by two concentric circles, the smaller symbolizing the learning process and the larger the developmental process evoked by learning.

Once a child has learned to perform an operation, he thus assimilates some structural principle whose sphere of application is other than just the operations of the type on whose basis the principle was assimilated. Consequently, in making one step in learning, a child makes two steps in development, that is, learning and development do not coincide. This concept is the essential aspect of the third group of theories we have discussed.

ZONE OF PROXIMAL DEVELOPMENT:
A NEW APPROACH

Although we reject all three theoretical positions discussed above, analyzing them leads us to a more adequate view of the relation between learning and development. The question to be framed in arriving at a solution to this problem is complex. It consists of two separate issues: first, the general relation between learning and development; and second, the specific features of this relationship when children reach school age.

That children's learning begins long before they attend school is the starting point of this discussion. Any learning a child encounters in school always has a previous history. For example, children begin to study arithmetic in school, but long beforehand they have had some experience with quantity—they have had to deal with operations of division, addition, subtraction, and determination of size. Consequently, children have their own preschool arithmetic, which only myopic psychologists could ignore.

It goes without saying that learning as it occurs in the preschool years differs markedly from school learning, which is concerned with the assimilation of the fundamentals of scientific knowledge. But even when, in the period of her first questions, a child assimilates the names of objects in her environment, she is learning. Indeed, can it be doubted that children learn speech from adults; or that, through asking questions and giving answers, children acquire a variety of information; or that, through imitating adults and through being instructed about how to act, children develop an entire repository of skills? Learning and development are interrelated from the child's very first day of life.

Koffka, attempting to clarify the laws of child learning and their relation to mental development, concentrates his attention on the simplest learning processes, those that occur in the preschool years. His error is that, while seeing a similarity between preschool and school learning, he fails to discern the difference—he does not see the specifically new elements that school learning introduces. He and others assume that the difference between preschool and school learning consists of nonsystematic learning in one case and systematic learning in the other. But "systematicness" is not the only issue; there is also the fact that school learning introduces something fundamentally new into the child's development. In order to elaborate the dimensions of school learning, we will describe a new and exceptionally important concept without which the issue cannot be resolved: the zone of proximal development.

A well known and empirically established fact is that learning should be matched in some manner with the child's developmental level. For example, it has been established that the teaching of reading, writing, and arithmetic should be initiated at a specific age level. Only recently, however, has attention been directed to the fact that we cannot limit ourselves merely to determining developmental levels if we wish to discover the actual relations of the developmental process to learning capabilities. We must determine at least two developmental levels.

The first level can be called the *actual developmental level,* that is, the level of development of a child's mental functions that has been established as a result of certain already *completed* developmental cycles. When we determine a child's mental age by using tests, we are almost always dealing with the actual developmental level. In studies of children's mental development it is generally assumed that only those things that children can do on their own are indicative of mental abilities. We give children a battery of tests or a variety of tasks of varying degrees of difficulty, and we judge the extent of their mental development on the basis of how they solve them and at what level of difficulty. On the other hand, if we offer leading questions or show how the problem is to be solved and the child then solves it, or if the teacher initiates the solution and the child completes it or solves it in collaboration with other children—in short, if the child barely misses an independent solution of the problem—the solution is not regarded as indicative of his mental development. This "truth" was familiar and reinforced by common sense. Over a decade even the profoundest thinkers never questioned the assumption; they never entertained the notion that what children can do with the assistance of others might be in some sense even more indicative of their mental development than what they can do alone.

Let us take a simple example. Suppose I investigate two children upon entrance into school, both of whom are ten years old chronologically and eight years old in terms of mental development. Can I say that they are the same age mentally? Of course. What does this mean? It means that they can independently deal with tasks up to the degree of difficulty that has been standardized for the eight-year-old level. If I stop at this point, people would imagine that the subsequent course of mental development and of school learning for these children will be the same, because it depends on their intellect. Of course, there may be other factors, for example, if one child was sick for half a year while the other was never absent from school; but generally speaking, the fate of these children should be the same. Now imagine that I do not terminate my study at this point, but only begin it. These children seem to be capable of handling problems up to an eight-year-old's level, but not beyond that. Suppose that I show them various ways of dealing with the problem. Different experimenters might employ different modes of demonstration in different cases: some might run through an entire demonstration and ask the children to repeat it, others might initiate the solution and ask the child to finish it, or offer leading questions. In short, in some way or another I propose that the children solve the problem with my assistance. Under these circumstances it turns out that the first child can deal with problems up to a twelve-year-old's level, the second up to a nine-year-old's. Now, are these children mentally the same?

When it was first shown that the capability of children with equal levels of mental development to learn under a teacher's guidance varied to a high degree, it became apparent that those children were not mentally the same age and that the subsequent course of their learning would obviously be different. This difference between twelve and eight, or between nine and eight, is what we call *the zone of proximal development. It is the distance between the actual developmental level as determined by independent problem solving and the level of potential development as determined through problem solving under adult guidance or in collaboration with more capable peers.*

If we naively ask what the actual developmental level is, or, to put it more simply, what more independent problem solving reveals, the most common answer would be that a child's actual developmental level defines functions that have already matured, that is, the end products of development. If a child can do such-and-such independently, it means that the functions for such-and-such have matured in her. What, then, is defined by the zone of proximal development, as determined through problems that children cannot solve independently but only with assistance? The zone of proximal development defines those functions that have not yet matured but are in the process of maturation, functions that will mature tomorrow but are currently in an embryonic state. These functions could be termed the "buds" or "flowers" of development rather than the "fruits" of development. The actual developmental level characterizes mental development retrospectively, while the zone of proximal development characterizes mental development prospectively.

The zone of proximal development furnishes psychologists and educators with a tool through which the internal course of development can be understood. By using this method we can take account of not only the cycles and maturation processes that have already been completed but also those processes that are currently in a state of formation, that are just beginning to mature and develop. Thus, the zone of proximal development permits us to delineate the child's immediate future and his dynamic developmental state, allowing not only for what already has been achieved developmentally but also for what is in the course of maturing. The two children in our example displayed the same mental age from the viewpoint of developmental cycles already completed, but the developmental dynamics of the two were entirely different. The state of a child's mental development can be determined only by clarifying its two levels: the actual developmental level and the zone of proximal development.

I will discuss one study of preschool children to demonstrate that what is in the zone of proximal development today will be the actual developmental level tomorrow—that is, what a child can do with assistance today she will be able to do by herself tomorrow.

The American researcher Dorothea McCarthy showed that among children between the ages of three and five there are two groups of functions: those the children already possess, and those they can perform under guidance, in groups, and in collaboration with one another but which they have not mastered independently. McCarthy's study demonstrated that this second group of functions is at the actual developmental level of five-to-seven-year-olds. What her subjects could do only under guidance, in collaboration, and in groups at the age of three-to-five years they could do independently when they reached the age of five-to-seven years.[5] Thus, if we were to determine only mental age—that is, only functions that have matured—we would have but a summary of completed development, while if we determine the maturing functions, we can predict what will happen to these children between five and seven, provided the same developmental conditions are maintained. The zone of proximal development can become a powerful concept in developmental research, one that can markedly enhance the effectiveness and utility of the application of diagnostics of mental development to educational problems.

A full understanding of the concept of the zone of proximal development must result in reevaluation of the role of imitation in learning. An unshakable tenet of classical psychology is that only the independent activity of children, not their imitative activity, indicates their level of mental development. This view is expressed in all current testing systems. In evaluating mental development, consideration is given to only those solutions to test problems which the child reaches without the assistance of others, without demonstrations, and without leading questions. Imitation and learning are thought of as purely mechanical processes. But recently psychologists have shown that a person can imitate only that which is within her developmental level. For example, if a child is having difficulty with a problem in arithmetic and the teacher solves it on the blackboard, the child may grasp the solution in an instant. But if the teacher were to solve a problem in higher mathematics, the child would not be able to understand the solution no matter how many times she imitated it.

Animal psychologists, and in particular Köhler, have dealt with this question of imitation quite well.[6] Köhler's experiments sought to determine whether primates are capable of graphic thought. The principal question was whether primates solved problems independently or whether they merely imitated solutions they had seen performed earlier, for example, watching other animals or humans use sticks and other tools and then imitating them. Köhler's special experiments, designed to determine what primates could imitate, reveal that primates can use imitation to solve only those problems that are of the same degree of difficulty as those they can solve alone. However, Köhler failed to take account of an important fact, namely, that primates cannot be taught (in the human sense of the word) through imitation, nor can their intellect be developed, because they have no zone of proximal development. A primate can learn a great deal through training by using its mechanical and mental skills, but it cannot be made more intelligent, that is, it cannot be taught to solve a variety of more advanced problems independently. For this reason animals are incapable of learning in the human sense of the term; *human learning presupposes a specific social nature and a process by which children grow into the intellectual life of those around them.*

Children can imitate a variety of actions that go well beyond the limits of their own capabilities. Using imitation, children are capable of doing much more in collective activity or under the guidance of adults. This fact, which seems to be of little significance in itself, is of fundamental importance in that it demands a radical alteration of the entire doctrine concerning the relation between learning and development in children. One direct consequence is a change in conclusions that may be drawn from diagnostic tests of development.

Formerly, it was believed that by using tests, we determine the mental development level with which education should reckon and whose limits it should not exceed. This procedure oriented learning toward yesterday's development, toward developmental stages already completed. The error of this view was discovered earlier in practice than in theory. It is demonstrated most clearly in the teaching of mentally retarded children. Studies have established that mentally retarded children are not very capable of abstract thinking. From this the pedagogy of the special school drew the seemingly correct conclusion that all teaching of such children should be based on the use of concrete, look-and-do methods. And yet a considerable amount of experience with this method resulted in profound disillusionment. It turned out that a teaching system based solely on concreteness—one that eliminated from teaching everything associated with abstract thinking—not only failed to help retarded children overcome their innate handicaps but also reinforced their handicaps by accustoming children exclusively to concrete thinking and thus suppressing the rudiments of any abstract thought that such children still have. Precisely because retarded children, when left to themselves, will never achieve well-elaborated forms of abstract thought, the school should make every effort to push them in that direction and to develop in them what is intrinsically lacking in their own development. In the current practices of special schools for retarded children, we can observe a beneficial shift away from this concept of concreteness, one that restores look-and-do methods to their proper role. Concreteness is now seen as necessary and unavoidable only as a stepping stone for developing abstract thinking—as a means, not as an end in itself.

Similarly, in normal children, learning which is oriented toward developmental levels that have already been reached is ineffective from the viewpoint of a child's overall development. It does not aim for a new stage of the developmental process but rather lags behind this process. Thus, the notion of a zone of proximal development enables us to propound a new formula, namely that the only "good learning" is that which is in advance of development.

The acquisition of language can provide a paradigm for the entire problem of the relation between learning and development. Language arises initially as a means of communication between the child and the people in his environment. Only subsequently, upon conversion to internal speech, does it come to organize the child's thought, that is, become an internal mental function. Piaget and others have shown that reasoning occurs in a children's group as an argument intended to prove one's own point of view before it occurs as an internal activity whose distinctive feature is that the child begins to perceive and check the basis of his thoughts. Such observations prompted Piaget to conclude that communication produces the need for checking and confirming thoughts, a process that is characteristic of adult thought.[7] In the same way that internal speech and reflective thought arise from the interactions between the child and persons in her environment, these interactions provide the source of development of a child's voluntary behavior. Piaget has shown that cooperation provides the basis for the development of a child's moral judgment. Earlier research established that a child first becomes able to subordinate her behavior to rules in group play and only later does voluntary self-regulation of behavior arise as an internal function.

These individual examples illustrate a general developmental law for the higher mental functions that we feel can be applied in its entirety to children's learning processes. We propose that an essential feature of learning is that it creates the zone of proximal development; that is, learning awakens a variety of internal developmental processes that are able to operate only when the child is interacting with people in his environment and in cooperation with his peers. Once these processes are internalized, they become part of the child's independent developmental achievement.

From this point of view, learning is not development; however, properly organized learning results in mental development and sets in motion a variety of developmental processes that would be impossible apart from learning. Thus, learning is a necessary and universal aspect of the process of developing culturally organized, specifically human, psychological functions.

To summarize, the most essential feature of our hypothesis is the notion that developmental processes do not coincide with learning processes. Rather, the developmental process lags behind the learning process; this sequence then results in zones of proximal development. Our analysis alters the traditional view that at the moment a child assimilates the meaning of a word, or masters an operation such as addition or written language, her developmental processes are basically completed. In fact, they have only just begun at that moment. The major consequence of analyzing the educational process in this manner is to show that the initial mastery of, for example, the four arithmetic operations provides the basis for the subsequent development of a variety of highly complex internal processes in children's thinking.

Our hypothesis establishes the unity but not the identity of learning processes and internal developmental processes. It presupposes that the one is converted into the other. Therefore, it becomes an important concern of psychological research to show how external knowledge and abilities in children become internalized.

Any investigation explores some sphere of reality. An aim of the psychological analysis of development is to describe the internal relations of the intellectual processes awakened by school learning. In this respect, such analysis will be directed inward and is analogous to the use of x-rays. If successful, it should reveal to the teacher how developmental processes stimulated by the course of school learning are carried through inside the head of each individual child. The revelation of this internal, subterranean developmental network of school subjects is a task of primary importance for psychological and educational analysis.

A second essential feature of our hypothesis is the notion that, although learning is directly related to the course of child development, the two are never accomplished in equal measure or in parallel. Development in children never follows school learning the way a shadow follows the object that casts it. In actuality, there are highly complex dynamic relations between developmental and learning processes that cannot be encompassed by an unchanging hypothetical formulation.

Each school subject has its own specific relation to the course of child development, a relation that varies as the child goes from one stage to another. This leads us directly to a reexamination of the problem of formal discipline, that is, to the significance of each particular subject from the viewpoint of overall mental development. Clearly, the problem cannot be solved by using any one formula; extensive and highly diverse concrete research based on the concept of the zone of proximal development is necessary to resolve the issue.

The Role of Play
in Development

To define play as an activity that gives pleasure to the child is inaccurate for two reasons. First, many activities give the child much keener experiences of pleasure than play, for example, sucking a pacifier, even though the child is not being satiated. And second, there are games in which the activity itself is not pleasurable, for example, games, predominantly at the end of preschool and the beginning of school age, that give pleasure only if the child finds the result interesting. Sporting games (not only athletic sports, but other games that can be won or lost) are very often accompanied by displeasure when the outcome is unfavorable to the child.

But while pleasure cannot be regarded as the defining characteristic of play, it seems to me that theories which ignore the fact that play fulfills children's needs result in a pedantic intellectualization of play. In speaking of child development in more general terms, many theorists mistakenly disregard the child's needs—understood in the broadest sense to include everything that is a motive for action. We often describe a child's development as the development of his intellectual functions; every child stands before us as a theoretician who, characterized by a higher or lower level of intellectual development, moves from one stage to another. But if we ignore the child's needs, and the incentives which are effective in getting him to act, we will never be able to understand his advance from one developmental stage to the next, because every advance is connected with a marked change in motives, inclinations, and incentives. That which is of the greatest interest to the infant has almost ceased to interest the toddler. The maturing of needs is a dominant issue in this discussion because it is impossible to ignore the

fact that the child satisfies certain needs in play. If we do not understand the special character of these needs, we cannot understand the
uniqueness of play as a form of activity.

A very young child tends to gratify her desires immediately; normally the interval between a desire and its fulfillment is extremely short.
No one has met a child under three years old who wants to do something
a few days in the future. However, at the preschool age, a great many
unrealizable tendencies and desires emerge. It is my belief that if needs
that could not be realized immediately did not develop during the school
years, there would be no play, because play seems to be invented at the
point when the child begins to experience unrealizable tendencies. Suppose that a very young (perhaps two-and-a-half-year-old) child wants
something—for example, to occupy her mother's role. She wants it at
once. If she cannot have it, she may throw a temper tantrum, but she
can usually be sidetracked and pacified so that she forgets her desire.
Toward the beginning of preschool age, when desires that cannot be
immediately gratified or forgotten make their appearance and the tendency to immediate fulfillment of desires, characteristic of the preceding
stage, is retained, the child's behavior changes. To resolve this tension,
the preschool child enters an imaginary, illusory world in which the
unrealizable desires can be realized, and this world is what we call
play. Imagination is a new psychological process for the child; it is not
present in the consciousness of the very young child, is totally absent in
animals, and represents a specifically human form of conscious activity.
Like all functions of consciousness, it originally arises from action. The
old adage that child's play is imagination in action must be reversed:
we can say that imagination in adolescents and school children is play
without action.

From this perspective it is clear that the pleasure derived from
preschool play is controlled by different motives than simple sucking
on a pacifier. This is not to say that play arises as the result of every
unsatisfied desire (as when, for example, the child wants to ride in the
cab, but the wish is not immediately gratified, so the child goes into her
room and pretends she is riding in a cab). It rarely happens in just this
way. Nor does the presence of such generalized emotions in play mean
that the child herself understands the motives giving rise to the game.
In this respect play differs substantially from work and other forms of
activity.

Thus, in establishing criteria for distinguishing a child's play from
other forms of activity, we conclude that in play a child creates an
imaginary situation. This is not a new idea, in the sense that imaginary

situations in play have always been recognized; but they were previously regarded as only one example of play activities. The imaginary situation was not considered the defining characteristic of play in general but was treated as an attribute of specific subcategories of play.

I find previous ideas unsatisfactory in three respects. First, if play is understood as symbolic, there is the danger that it might come to be viewed as an activity akin to algebra; that is, play, like algebra, might be considered a system of signs that generalize reality, with no characteristics that I consider specific to play. The child would be seen as an unsuccessful algebraist who cannot yet write the symbols but can depict them in action. I believe that play is not symbolic action in the proper sense of the term, so it becomes essential to show the role of motivation in play. Second, this argument stressing the importance of cognitive processes neglects not only the motivation for, but also the circumstances of, the child's activity. And third, previous approaches do not help us to understand the role of play in later development.

If all play is really the realization in play form of tendencies that cannot be immediately gratified, then elements of imaginary situations will automatically be a part of the emotional tone of play itself. Consider the child's activity during play. What does a child's behavior in an imaginary situation mean? We know that the development of playing games with rules begins in the late preschool period and develops during school age. A number of investigators, although not belonging to the camp of dialectical materialists, have approached this issue along the lines recommended by Marx when he said that "the anatomy of man is the key to the anatomy of the ape." They have begun their examination of early play in the light of later rule-based play and have concluded from this that play involving an imaginary situation is, in fact, rule-based play.

One could go even further and propose that there is no such thing as play without rules. The imaginary situation of any form of play already contains rules of behavior, although it may not be a game with formulated rules laid down in advance. The child imagines himself to be the mother and the doll to be the child, so he must obey the rules of maternal behavior. Sully early noted that, remarkably, young children could make the play situation and reality coincide.[1] He described a case where two sisters, aged five and seven, said to each other, "Let's play sisters." They were playing at reality. In certain cases, I have found it easy to elicit such play in children. It is very easy, for example, to have a child play at being a child while the mother is playing the role of mother, that is, playing at what is actually true. The vital difference, as Sully describes it, is that the child in playing tries to be what she thinks a sister should be. In life the child behaves without thinking that she is her sister's sister. In the game of sisters playing at "sisters," however, they are both concerned with displaying their sisterhood; the fact that two sisters decided to play sisters induces them both to acquire rules of behavior. Only actions that fit these rules are acceptable to the play situation: they dress alike, talk alike, in short, they enact whatever emphasizes their relationship as sisters vis-à-vis adults and strangers. The elder, holding the younger by the hand, may keep telling her about other people: "That is theirs, not ours." This means: "My sister and I act the same, we are treated the same, but others are treated differently." In this example the emphasis is on the sameness of everything that is connected with the child's concept of a sister; as a result of playing, the child comes to understand that sisters possess a different relationship to each other than to other people. What passes unnoticed by the child in real life becomes a rule of behavior in play.

What would remain if play were structured in such a way that there were no imaginary situation? The rules would remain. Whenever there is an imaginary situation in play, there are rules—not rules that are formulated in advance and change during the course of the game but ones that stem from an imaginary situation. Therefore, the notion that a child can behave in an imaginary situation without rules is simply inaccurate. If the child is playing the role of a mother, then she has rules of maternal behavior. The role the child fulfills, and her relation to the object (if the object has changed its meaning), will always stem from the rules.

At first it seemed that the investigator's only task in analyzing play was to disclose the hidden rules in all play, but it has been demonstrated that the so-called pure games with rules are essentially games with imaginary situations. Just as the imaginary situation has to contain rules of behavior, so every game with rules contains an imaginary situation. For example, playing chess creates an imaginary situation. Why? Because the knight, king, queen, and so forth can only move in specified ways; because covering and taking pieces are purely chess concepts. Although in the chess game there is no direct substitute for real-life relationships, it is a kind of imaginary situation nevertheless. The simplest game with rules immediately turns into an imaginary situation in the sense that as soon as the game is regulated by certain rules, a number of possibilities for action are ruled out.

Just as we were able to show at the beginning that every imaginary situation contains rules in a concealed form, we have also demonstrated the reverse—that every game with rules contains an imaginary situation in a concealed form. The development from games with an overt imaginary situation and covert rules to games with overt rules and a covert imaginary situation outlines the evolution of children's play.

ACTION AND MEANING IN PLAY

The influence of play on a child's development is enormous. Play in an imaginary situation is essentially impossible for a child under three in that it is a novel form of behavior liberating the child from constraints. To a considerable extent the behavior of a very young child—and to an absolute extent, that of an infant—is determined by the conditions in which the activity takes place, as the experiments of Lewin and others have shown.[2] For example, Lewin's demonstration of the great difficulty a small child has in realizing that he must first turn his back to a stone in order to sit on it illustrates the extent to which a very young child is bound in every action by situational constraints. It is hard to imagine a greater contrast to Lewin's experiments showing the situational constraints on activity than what we observe in play. It is here that the child learns to act in a cognitive, rather than an externally visual, realm by relying on internal tendencies and motives and not on incentives supplied by external things. A study by Lewin on the motivating nature of things for a very young child concludes that *things* dictate to the child what he must do: a door demands to be opened and closed, a staircase to be climbed, a bell to be rung. In short, things have such an inherent motivating force with respect to a very young child's actions and so extensively determine the child's behavior that Lewin arrived at the notion of creating a psychological topology: he expressed mathematically the trajectory of the child's movement in a field according to the distribution of things with varying attracting or repelling forces.

The root of situational constraints upon a child lies in a central fact of consciousness characteristic of early childhood: the union of motives and perception. At this age perception is generally not an independent but rather an integrated feature of a motor reaction. Every perception is a stimulus to activity. Since a situation is communicated psychologically through perception, and since perception is not separated from motivational and motor activity, it is understandable that with her consciousness so structured, the child is constrained by the situation in which she finds herself.

But in play, things lose their determining force. *The child sees one thing but acts differently in relation to what he sees. Thus, a condition is reached in which the child begins to act independently of what he sees.* Certain brain-damaged patients lose the ability to act independently of what they see. In considering such patients one can appreciate that the freedom of action adults and more mature children enjoy is not acquired in a flash but has to go through a long process of development.

Action in an imaginary situation teaches the child to guide her behavior not only by immediate perception of objects or by the situation immediately affecting her but also by the meaning of this situation. Experiments and day-to-day observation clearly show that *it is impossible for very young children to separate the field of meaning from the visual field* because there is such intimate fusion between meaning and what is seen. Even a child of two years, when asked to repeat the sentence "Tanya is standing up" when Tanya is sitting in front of her, will change it to "Tanya is sitting down." In certain diseases, exactly the same situation is encountered. Goldstein and Gelb described a number of patients who were unable to state something that was not true.[3] Gelb has data on one patient who was left-handed and incapable of writing the sentence "I can write well with my right hand." When looking out of the window on a fine day he was unable to repeat "The weather is nasty today," but would say "The weather is fine." Often we find that a patient with a speech disturbance is incapable of repeating senseless phrases, for example, "Snow is black," while other phrases equally difficult in their grammatical and semantic construction can be repeated. This tie between perception and meaning can be seen in the process of children's speech development. You say to the child, "clock," and he starts looking for the clock. The word originally signifies a particular spatial location.

A divergence between the fields of meaning and vision first occurs at preschool age. In play thought is separated from objects and action arises from ideas rather than from things: a piece of wood begins to be a doll and a stick becomes a horse. Action according to rules begins to be determined by ideas and not by objects themselves. This is such a reversal of the child's relation to the real, immediate, concrete situation that it is hard to underestimate its full significance. The child does not do this all at once because it is terribly difficult for a child to sever thought (the meaning of a word) from object.

Play provides a transitional stage in this direction whenever an object (for example, a stick) becomes a pivot for severing the meaning of horse from a real horse. The child cannot as yet detach thought from object. The child's weakness is that in order to imagine a horse, he needs to define his action by means of using "the-horse-in-the-stick" as the pivot. But all the same, the basic structure determining the child's relation to reality is radically changed at this crucial point, because the structure of his perceptions changes.

As I discussed in earlier chapters, a special feature of human perception (one arising at a very early age) is the so-called perception of real objects, that is, the perception of not only colors and shapes, but also meaning. This is something to which there is no analogy in animal perception. Humans do not merely see something round and black with two hands; they see a clock and can distinguish one thing from another. Thus, the structure of human perception could be figuratively expressed as a ratio in which the object is the numerator and the meaning is the denominator (object/meaning). This ratio symbolizes the idea that all human perception is made up of generalized rather than isolated perceptions. For the child the object dominates in the object/meaning ratio and meaning is subordinated to it. At the crucial moment when a stick becomes the pivot for detaching the meaning of horse from a real horse, this ratio is inverted and meaning predominates, giving meaning/object.

This is not to say that properties of things as such have no meaning. Any stick can be a horse but, for example, a postcard cannot be a horse for a child. Goethe's contention that in play any thing can be anything for a child is incorrect. Of course, for adults who can make conscious use of symbols, a postcard *can* be a horse. If I want to show the location of something, I can put down a match and say, "This is a horse." That would be enough. For a child it cannot be a horse because one must use a stick; because of the lack of free substitution, the child's activity is play and not symbolism. A symbol is a sign, but the stick does not function as the sign of a horse for the child, who retains the properties of things but changes their meaning. Their meaning, in play, becomes the central point and objects are moved from a dominant to a subordinate position.

The child at play operates with meanings detached from their usual objects and actions; however, a highly interesting contradiction arises in which he fuses real actions and real objects. This characterizes the transitional nature of play; it is a stage between the purely situational constraints of early childhood and adult thought, which can be totally free of real situations.

When the stick becomes the pivot for detaching the meaning of "horse" from a real horse, the child makes one object influence another semantically. He cannot detach meaning from an object, or a word from an object, except by finding a pivot in something else. Transfer of meanings is facilitated by the fact that the child accepts a word as the property of a thing; he sees not the word but the thing it designates. For a child, the word "horse" applied to the stick means "there is a horse," because mentally he sees the object standing behind the word. A vital transitional stage toward operating with meanings occurs when a child first acts with meanings as with objects (as when he acts with the stick as though it were a horse). Later he carries out these acts consciously. This change is seen, too, in the fact that before a child has acquired grammatical and written language, he knows how to do things but does not know that he knows. He does not master these activities voluntarily. In play a child spontaneously makes use of his ability to separate meaning from an object without knowing he is doing it, just as he does not know he is speaking in prose but talks without paying attention to the words. Thus, through play the child achieves a functional definition of concepts or objects, and words become parts of a thing.

The creation of an imaginary situation is not a fortuitous fact in a child's life, but is rather the first manifestation of the child's emancipation from situational constraints. The primary paradox of play is that the child operates with an alienated meaning in a real situation. The second paradox is that in play she adopts the line of least resistance—she does what she most feels like doing because play is connected with pleasure —and at the same time she learns to follow the line of greatest resistance by subordinating herself to rules and thereby renouncing what she wants, since subjection to rules and renunciation of impulsive action constitute the path to maximum pleasure in play.

Play continually creates demands on the child to act against immediate impulse. At every step the child is faced with a conflict between the rules of the game and what he would do if he could suddenly act spontaneously. In the game he acts counter to the way he wants to act. A child's greatest self-control occurs in play. He achieves the maximum display of willpower when he renounces an immediate attraction in the game (such as candy, which by the rules of the game he is forbidden to eat because it represents something inedible). Ordinarily a child experiences subordination to rules in the renunciation of something he wants, but here subordination to a rule and renunciation of action on immediate impulse are the means to maximum pleasure.

Thus, the essential attribute of play is a rule that has become a desire. Spinoza's notions of "an idea which has become a desire, a concept which has turned into a passion" finds its prototype in play, which is the realm of spontaneity and freedom. To carry out the rule is a source of pleasure. The rule wins because it is the strongest impulse. Such a rule is an internal rule, a rule of self-restraint and self-determination, as Piaget says, and not a rule the child obeys like a physical law. In short, *play gives a child a new form of desires*. It teaches her to desire by relating her desires to a fictitious "I," to her role in the game and its rules. In this way a child's greatest achievements are possible in play, achievements that tomorrow will become her basic level of real action and morality.

SEPARATING ACTION AND MEANING

Now we can say the same thing about the child's activity that we said about objects. Just as we had the $\frac{object}{meaning}$ ratio, we also have the $\frac{action}{meaning}$ ratio. Whereas action dominates early in development, this structure is inverted; meaning becomes the numerator, while action takes the place of the denominator.

In a child of preschool age, action is initially dominant over meaning and is incompletely understood. The child is able to do more than he can understand. But it is at this age that an action structure first arises in which meaning is the determinant, although meaning must influence the child's behavior within constraints provided by structural features of the action. Children, in playing at eating from a plate, have been shown to perform actions with their hands reminiscent of real eating, while all actions that did not designate eating were impossible. Throwing one's hands back instead of stretching them toward the plate turned out to be impossible, for such an action would have a destructive effect on the game. A child does not behave in a purely symbolic fashion in play; rather he wishes and realizes his wishes by letting the basic categories of reality pass through his experience. The child, in wishing, carries out his wishes. In thinking, he acts. Internal and external action are inseparable: imagination, interpretation, and will are the internal processes carried by external action. What was said about detaching meaning from objects applies equally well to the child's own actions. A child who stamps on the ground and imagines herself riding a horse has thereby inverted the $\frac{action}{meaning}$ ratio to $\frac{meaning}{action}$.

The developmental history of the relation between meaning and action is analogous to the development history of the meaning/object relation. In order to detach the meaning of the action from the real action (riding a horse, without the opportunity to do so), the child requires a pivot in the form of an action to replace the real one. While action begins as the numerator of the $\frac{action}{meaning}$ structure, now the structure is inverted and meaning becomes the numerator. Action retreats to second place and becomes the pivot; meaning is again detached from action by means of a different action. This is another example of the way in which human behavior comes to depend upon operations based on meanings where the motive that initiates the behavior is sharply separated from fulfillment. The separation of meaning from objects and action has different consequences, however. Just as operating with the meaning of *things* leads to abstract thought, we find that the development of will, the ability to make conscious choices, occurs when the child operates with the meaning of *actions*. In play, an action replaces another action just as an object replaces another object.

How does the child float from one object to another, from one action to another? This is accomplished by movement in the field of meaning— which subordinates all real objects and actions to itself. Behavior is not bound by the immediate perceptual field. This movement in the field of meaning predominates in play. On the one hand, it represents movement in an abstract field (which thus makes an appearance in play prior to the appearance of voluntary operation with meanings). On the other hand, the method of movement is situational and concrete. (It is an affective, not a logical change). In other words, the field of meaning appears, but action within it occurs just as in reality. Herein lies the main developmental contradiction of play.

CONCLUSION

I would like to close this discussion of play by first showing that play is not the predominant feature of childhood but it is a leading factor in development. Second, I want to demonstrate the significance of the change from predominance of the imaginary situation to predominance of rules in the development of play itself. And third, I want to point out internal transformations in the child's development brought about by play.

How does play relate to development? In fundamental, everyday situations a child's behavior is the opposite of his behavior in play. In play, action is subordinated to meaning, but in real life, of course, action dominates meaning. Therefore, to consider play as the prototype of a child's everyday activity and its predominant form is completely incorrect.

This is the main flaw in Koffka's theory. He considers play as the child's other world.[4] Everything that concerns a child is play reality, while everything that concerns an adult is serious reality. A given object has one meaning in play and another outside of it. In a child's world the logic of wishes and of satisfying urges dominates, and not real logic. The illusory nature of play is transferred to life. This would all be true if play were indeed the predominant form of a child's activity. But it is difficult to accept the insane picture that comes to mind if the form of activity we have been speaking of were to become the predominant form of a child's everyday activity, even if only partially transferred to real life.

Koffka gives a number of examples to show how a child transfers a situation from play into life. But the ubiquitous transference of play behavior to real life could only be regarded as an unhealthy symptom. To behave in a real situation as in an illusory one is the first sign of delirium. Play behavior in real life is normally seen only in the type of game when children begin to play at what they are in fact doing, evidently creating associations that facilitate the execution of an unpleasant action (as when children who do not want to go to bed say, "Let's play that it's nighttime and we have to go to sleep"). Thus, it seems to me that play is not the predominant type of activity at preschool age. Only theories which maintain that a child does not have to satisfy the basic requirements of life but can live in search of pleasure could possibly suggest that a child's world is a play world.

Looking at the matter from the opposite perspective, could one suppose that a child's behavior is always guided by meaning, that a preschooler's behavior is so arid that he never behaves spontaneously simply because he thinks he should behave otherwise? This strict subordination to rules is quite impossible in life, but in play it does become possible: thus, play creates a zone of proximal development of the child. In play a child always behaves beyond his average age, above his daily behavior; in play it is as though he were a head taller than himself. As in the focus of a magnifying glass, play contains all developmental tendencies in a condensed form and is itself a major source of development.

Though the play–development relationship can be compared to the instruction–development relationship, play provides a much wider background for changes in needs and consciousness. Action in the imaginative sphere, in an imaginary situation, the creation of voluntary intentions, and the formation of real-life plans and volitional motives—all appear in play and make it the highest level of preschool development.

question for students

The child moves forward essentially through play activity. Only in this sense can play be considered a leading activity that determines the child's development.

How does play change? It is remarkable that the child starts with an imaginary situation that initially is so very close to the real one. A reproduction of the real situation takes place. For example, a child playing with a doll repeats almost exactly what his mother does with him. This means that in the original situation rules operate in a condensed and compressed form. There is very little of the imaginary. It is an imaginary situation, but it is only comprehensible in the light of a real situation that has just occurred. Play is more nearly recollection of something that has actually happened than imagination. It is more memory in action than a novel imaginary situation.

As play develops, we see a movement toward the conscious realization of its purpose. It is incorrect to conceive of play as activity without purpose. In athletic games one can win or lose; in a race one can come in first, second, or last. In short, the purpose decides the game and justifies the activity. Purpose, as the ultimate goal, determines the child's affective attitude to play. When running a race, a child can be highly agitated or distressed and little pleasure may remain because she finds it physically painful to run, and if she is overtaken she will experience little functional pleasure. In sports the purpose of the game is one of its dominant features, without which there would be no point—like examining a piece of candy, putting it into one's mouth, chewing it, and then spitting it out. In such play, the object, which is to win, is recognized in advance.

At the end of development, rules emerge, and the more rigid they are the greater the demands on the child's application, the greater the regulation of the child's activity, the more tense and acute play becomes. Simply running around without purpose or rules is boring and does not appeal to children. Consequently, a complex of originally undeveloped features comes to the fore at the end of play development—features that had been secondary or incidental in the beginning occupy a central position at the end, and vice versa.

In one sense a child at play is free to determine his own actions. But in another sense this is an illusory freedom, for his actions are in fact subordinated to the meanings of things, and he acts accordingly.

From the point of view of development, creating an imaginary situation can be regarded as a means of developing abstract thought. The corresponding development of rules leads to actions on the basis of which the division between work and play becomes possible, a division encountered at school age as a fundamental fact.

As figuratively expressed by one investigator, play for a child under three is a serious game, just as it is for an adolescent, although, of course, in a different sense of the word; serious play for a very young child means that she plays without separating the imaginary situation from the real one. For the school child, play becomes a more limited form of activity, predominantly of the athletic type, which fills a specific role in the school child's development but lacks the significance of play for the preschooler. At school age play does not die away but permeates the attitude toward reality. It has its own inner continuation in school instruction and work (compulsory activity based on rules). It is the essence of play that a new relation is created between the field of meaning and the visual field—that is, between situations in thought and real situations.

Superficially, play bears little resemblance to the complex, mediated form of thought and volition it leads to. Only a profound internal analysis makes it possible to determine its course of change and its role in development.

8

The Prehistory of Written Language

Until now, writing has occupied too narrow a place in school practice as compared to the enormous role that it plays in children's cultural
development. The teaching of writing has been conceived in narrowly
practical terms. Children are taught to trace out letters and make words
out of them, but they are not taught written language. The mechanics of
reading what is written are so emphasized that they overshadow written
language as such.

Something similar has happened in teaching spoken language to
deaf-mutes. Attention has been concentrated entirely on correct production of particular letters and distinct articulation of them. In this case,
teachers of deaf-mutes have not discerned spoken language behind these
pronunciation techniques, and the result has been dead speech.

This situation is to be explained primarily by historical factors:
specifically, by the fact that practical pedagogy, despite the existence
of many methods for teaching reading and writing, has yet to work out
an effective, scientific procedure for teaching children written language.
Unlike the teaching of spoken language, into which children grow of
their own accord, teaching of written language is based on artificial
training. Such training requires an enormous amount of attention and
effort on the part of teacher and pupil and thus becomes something
self-contained, relegating living written language to the background.
Instead of being founded on the needs of children as they naturally
develop and on their own activity, writing is given to them from without,
from the teacher's hands. This situation recalls the development of a
technical skill such as piano-playing: the pupil develops finger dexterity

and learns to strike the keys while reading music, but he is in no way involved in the essence of the music itself.

Such one-sided enthusiasm for the mechanics of writing has had an impact not only on the practice of teaching but on the theoretical statement of the problem as well. Up to this point, psychology has conceived of writing as a complicated motor skill. It has paid remarkably little attention to the question of written language as such, that is, a particular system of symbols and signs whose mastery heralds a critical turning-point in the entire cultural development of the child.

A feature of this system is that it is second-order symbolism, which gradually becomes direct symbolism. This means that written language consists of a system of signs that designate the sounds and words of spoken language, which, in turn, are signs for real entities and relations. Gradually this intermediate link, spoken language, disappears, and written language is converted into a system of signs that directly symbolize the entities and relations between them. It seems clear that mastery of such a complex sign system cannot be accomplished in a purely mechanical and external manner; rather it is the culmination of a long process of development of complex behavioral functions in the child. Only by understanding the entire history of sign development in the child and the place of writing in it can we approach a correct solution of the psychology of writing.

The developmental history of written language, however, poses enormous difficulties for research. As far as we can judge from the available material, it does not follow a single direct line in which something like a clear continuity of forms is maintained. Instead, it offers the most unexpected metamorphoses, that is, transformations of particular forms of written language into others. To quote Baldwin's apt expression regarding the development of things, it is as much involution as evolution.[1] This means that, together with processes of development, forward motion, and appearance of new forms, we can discern processes of curtailment, disappearance, and reverse development of old forms at each step. The developmental history of written language among children is full of such discontinuities. Its line of development seems to disappear altogether; then suddenly, as if from nowhere, a new line begins, and at first it seems that there is absolutely no continuity between the old and the new. But only a naive view of development as a purely evolutionary process involving nothing but the gradual accumulation of small changes and the gradual conversion of one form into another can conceal from us the true nature of these processes. This revolutionary type of development is in no way new for science in general; it is new only for child psychology. Therefore, despite a few daring attempts, child psychology does not have a cogent view of the development of written language as a historical process, as a unified process of development.

The first task of a scientific investigation is to reveal this prehistory of children's written language, to show what leads children to writing, through what important points this prehistorical development passes, and in what relationship it stands to school learning. At the present time, in spite of a variety of research studies, we are in no position to write a coherent or complete history of written language in children. We can only discern the most important points in this development and discuss its major changes. This history begins with the appearance of the gesture as a visual sign for the child.

GESTURES AND VISUAL SIGNS

The gesture is the initial visual sign that contains the child's future writing as an acorn contains a future oak. Gestures, it has been correctly said, are writing in air, and written signs frequently are simply gestures that have been fixed.

Wurth pointed out the link between gesture and pictorial or pictographic writing in discussing the development of writing in human history.[2] He showed that figurative gestures often simply denote the reproduction of a graphic sign; on the other hand, signs are often the fixation of gestures. An indicating line employed in pictographic writing denotes the index finger in fixed position. All these symbolic designations in pictorial writing, according to Wurth, can be explained only by derivation from gesture language, even if they subsequently become detached from it and can function independently.

There are two other domains in which gestures are linked to the origin of written signs. The first concerns children's scribbles. We have observed in experiments on drawing that children frequently switch to dramatization, depicting by gestures what they should show on the drawing; the pencil-marks are only a supplement to this gestural representation. I could cite many instances. A child who has to depict running begins by depicting the motion with her fingers, and she regards the resultant marks and dots on paper as a representation of running. When she goes on to depict jumping, her hand begins to make movements depicting jumps; what appears on paper remains the same. In general, we are inclined to view children's first drawings and scribbles rather as gestures than as drawing in the true sense of the word. We are also inclined to ascribe to the same phenomenon the experimentally demonstrated fact that, in drawing complex objects, children do not render their parts but rather general qualities, such as an impression of roundness and so forth. When a child depicts a cylindrical can as a closed curve that resembles a circle, she thus depicts something round. This developmental phase coincides nicely with the general motor set that characterizes children of this age and governs the entire style and nature of their first drawings. Children behave in the same way in depicting concepts that are at all complex or abstract. Children do not draw, they indicate, and the pencil merely fixes the indicatory gesture. When asked to draw good weather, a child will indicate the bottom of the page by making a horizontal motion of the hand, explaining, "This is the earth," and then, after a number of confused upward hatchwise motions, "And this is good weather." We have had the occasion to verify more precisely, in experiments, the kinship between gestural depiction and depiction by drawing, and have obtained symbolic and graphic depiction through gestures in five-year-olds.

DEVELOPMENT OF SYMBOLISM IN PLAY

The second realm that links gestures and written language is children's games. For children some objects can readily denote others, replacing them and becoming signs for them, and the degree of similarity between a plaything and the object it denotes is unimportant. What is most important is the utilization of the plaything and the possibility of executing a representational gesture with it. This is the key to the entire symbolic function of children's play. A pile of clothes or piece of wood becomes a baby in a game because the same gestures that depict holding a baby in one's hands or feeding a baby can apply to them. The child's self-motion, his own gestures, are what assign the function of sign to the object and give it meaning. All symbolic representational activity is full of such indicatory gestures; for instance, a stick becomes a riding-horse for a child because it can be placed between the legs and a gesture can be employed that communicates that the stick designates a horse in this instance.

From this point of view, therefore, children's symbolic play can be understood as a very complex system of "speech" through gestures that communicate and indicate the meaning of playthings. It is only on the basis of these indicatory gestures that playthings themselves gradually acquire their meaning—just as drawing, while initially supported by gesture, becomes an independent sign.

We attempted experimentally to establish this particular special stage of object writing in children. We conducted play experiments in which, in a joking manner, we began to designate things and people involved in the play by familiar objects. For example, a book off to one side designated a house, keys meant children, a pencil meant a nurse-maid, a pocket watch a drugstore, a knife a doctor, an inkwell cover a horse-drawn carriage, and so forth. Then the children were given a simple story through figurative gestures involving these objects. They could read it with great ease. For example, a doctor arrives at a house in a carriage, knocks at the door, the nursemaid opens, he examines the children, he writes a prescription and leaves, the nursemaid goes to the drugstore, comes back, and administers medicine to the children. Most three-year-olds can read this symbolic notation with great ease. Four-or-five-year-olds can read more complex notation: a man is walking in the forest and is attacked by a wolf, which bites him; the man extricates himself by running, a doctor gives him aid, and he goes to the drugstore and then home; a hunter sets out for the forest to kill the wolf.

What is noteworthy is that perceptual similarity of objects plays no noticeable part in the understanding of the symbolic notation. All that matters is that the objects admit the appropriate gesture and can function as a point of application for it. Hence, things with which this gestural structure cannot be performed are absolutely rejected by children. For example, in this game, which is conducted at a table and which involves small items on the table, children will absolutely refuse to play if we take their fingers, put them on a book, and say, "Now, as a joke, these will be children." They object that there is no such game. Fingers are too connected with their own bodies for them to be an object for a corresponding indicatory gesture. In the same way, a piece of furniture in the room or one of the people in the game cannot become involved. The object itself performs a substitution function: a pencil substitutes for a nursemaid or a watch for a drugstore, but only the relevant gesture endows them with this meaning. However, under the influence of this gesture, older children begin to make one exceptionally important discovery—that objects can indicate the things they denote as well as substitute for them. For example, when we put down a book with a dark cover and say that this will be a forest, a child will spontaneously add, "Yes, it's a forest because it's black and dark." She thus isolates one of the features of the object, which for her is an indication of the fact that the book is supposed to mean a forest. In the same way, when a metal inkwell cover denotes a carriage, a child will point and say, "This is the seat." When a pocket watch is to denote a drugstore, one child might point to the numbers on the face and say, "This is medicine in the drugstore"; another might point to the ring and say, "This is the entrance." Referring to a bottle that is playing the part of a wolf, a child will point to the neck and say, "And this is his mouth." If the experimenter asks, pointing to the stopper, "And what is this?" the child answers, "He's caught the stopper and is holding it in his teeth."

In all these examples we see the same thing, namely, that the customary structure of things is modified under the impact of the new meaning it has acquired. In response to the fact that a watch denotes a drugstore, a feature of the watch is isolated and assumes the function of a new sign or indication of *how* the watch denotes a drugstore, either through the feature of medicine or of the entrance. The customary structure of things (stopper in a bottle) begins to be reflected in the new structure (wolf holds stopper in teeth), and this structural modification becomes so strong that in a number of experiments we sometimes instilled a particular symbolic meaning of an object in the children. For example, a pocket watch denoted a drugstore in all our play sessions. whereas other objects changed meaning rapidly and frequently. In taking up a new game, we would put down the same watch and explain, in accordance with the new procedures, "Now this is a bakery." One child immediately placed a pen edgewise across the watch, dividing it in half, and, indicating one half, said, "All right, here is the drugstore, and here is the bakery." The old meaning thus became independent and functioned as a means for a new one. We could also discern this acquisition of independent meaning outside the immediate game; if a knife fell, a child would exclaim, "The doctor has fallen." Thus, the object acquires a sign function with a developmental history of its own that is now independent of the child's gesture. This is second-order symbolism, and because it develops in play, we see make-believe play as a major contributor to the development of written language—a system of second-order symbolism.

As in play, so too in drawing, representation of meaning initially arises as first-order symbolism. As we have already pointed out, the first drawings arise from gestures of the (pencil-equipped) hand, and the gesture constitutes the first representation of meaning. Only later on does the graphic representation begin independently to denote some object. The nature of this relationship is that the marks already made on paper are given an appropriate name.

H. Hetzer undertook to study experimentally how symbolic representation of things—so important in learning to write—develops in three-to-six-year-old children.[3] Her experiments involved four basic series. The first investigated the function of symbols in children's play. Children were to portray, in play, a father or mother doing what they do in the course of a day. During this game a make-believe interpretation of particular objects was given, making it possible for the researcher to trace the symbolic function assigned to things during the game. The second series involved building materials, and the third involved drawing with colored pencils. Particular attention in both these experiments was paid to the point at which the appropriate meaning was named. The fourth series undertook to investigate, in the form of a game of post office, the extent to which children can perceive purely arbitrary combinations of signs. The game used pieces of paper of various colors to denote different types of mail: telegrams, newspapers, money orders, packages, letters, postcards, and so forth. Thus, the experiments explicitly related these different forms of activity, whose only common feature is that a symbolic function is involved in all of them, and attempted to link them all with the development of written language, as we did in our experiments.

Hetzer was able to show clearly which symbolic meanings arise in play via figurative gestures and which via words. Children's egocentric language was widely manifest in these games. Whereas some children depicted everything by using movements and mimicry, not employing speech as a symbolic resource at all, for other children actions were accompanied by speech: the child both spoke and acted. For a third group, purely verbal expression not supported by any activity began to predominate. Finally, a fourth group of children did not play at all, and speech became the sole mode of representation, with mimicry and gestures receding into the background. The percentage of purely play actions decreased with age, while speech gradually predominated. The most important conclusion drawn from this developmental investigation, as the author says, is that the difference in play activity between three-year-olds and six-year-olds is not in the perception of symbols but in the mode in which various forms of representation are used. In our opinion, this is a highly important conclusion; it indicates that symbolic representation in play is essentially a particular form of speech at an earlier stage, one which leads directly to written language.

As development proceeds, the general process of naming shifts farther and farther toward the beginning of the process, and thus the process itself is tantamount to the writing of a word that has just been named. Even a three-year-old understands the representational function of a toy construction, while a four-year-old names his creations even before he begins to construct them. Similarly, we see in drawing that a three-year-old is still unaware of the symbolic meaning of a drawing; it is only around age seven that all children master this completely. At the same time, our analysis of children's drawings definitely shows that, from the psychological point of view, we should regard such drawings as a particular kind of child speech.

DEVELOPMENT OF SYMBOLISM IN DRAWING

K. Buhler correctly notes that drawing begins in children when spoken speech has already made great progress and has become habitual.[4] Subsequently, he says, speech predominates in general and shapes the greater part of inner life in accordance with its laws. This includes drawing.

Children initially draw from memory. If asked to draw their mother sitting opposite them or some object before them, they draw without ever looking at the original—not what they see but what they know. Often children's drawings not only disregard but also directly contradict the actual perception of the object. We find what Buhler calls "x-ray drawings." A child will draw a clothed figure, but at the same time will include his legs, stomach, wallet in his pocket, and even the money in the wallet—that is, things he knows about but which cannot be seen in the case in question. In drawing a figure in profile, a child will add a second eye or will include a second leg on a horseman in profile. Finally, very important parts of the object will be omitted; for instance, a child will draw legs that grow straight out of the head, omitting the neck and torso, or will combine individual parts of a figure.

As Sully showed, children do not strive for representation; they are much more symbolists than naturalists and are in no way concerned with complete and exact similarity, desiring only the most superficial indications.[5] We cannot assume that children know people no better than they depict them; rather they try more to name and designate than to represent. A child's memory does not yield a simple depiction of representational images at this age. Rather, it yields predispositions to judgments that are invested with speech or capable of being so invested. We see that when a child unburdens his repository of memory in drawing, he does so in the mode of speech—telling a story. A major feature of this mode is a certain degree of abstraction, which any verbal representation necessarily entails. Thus we see that drawing is graphic speech that arises on the basis of verbal speech. The schemes that distinguish children's first drawings are reminiscent in this sense of verbal concepts that communicate only the essential features of objects. This gives us grounds for regarding children's drawing as a preliminary stage in the development of written language.

The further development of children's drawing, however, is not something self-understood and purely mechanical. There is a critical moment in going from simple mark-making on paper to the use of pencil-marks as signs that depict or mean something. All psychologists agree that the child must discover that the lines he makes can signify something. Sully illustrates this discovery using the example of a child who haphazardly drew a spiral line, without any meaning, suddenly grasped a certain similarity, and joyfully exclaimed, "Smoke, smoke!"

Although this process of recognizing what is drawn is encountered in early childhood, it is still not equivalent to the discovery of symbolic function, as observations have shown. Initially, even if a child perceives a similarity in a drawing, he takes the drawing to be an object that is similar or of the same kind, not as a representation or symbol of the object.

When a girl who was shown a drawing of her doll exclaimed, "A doll just like mine!" it is possible that she had in mind another object just like hers. According to Hetzer, there is no evidence that forces us to assume that assimilation of the drawing to an object means at the same time an understanding that the drawing is a representation of the object. For the girl, the drawing is not a representation of a doll but another doll just like hers. Proof of this is provided by the fact that for a long time children relate to drawings as if they were objects. For example, when a drawing shows a boy with his back to the observer, the child will turn the sheet over to try to see the face. Even among five-year-olds we always observed that, in response to the question, "Where is his face and nose?" children would turn the drawing over, and only then would answer, "It's not there, its's not drawn."

We feel that Hetzer is most justified in asserting that primary symbolic representation should be ascribed to speech, and that it is on the basis of speech that all the other sign systems are created. Indeed, the continuing shift toward the beginning in the moment of naming a drawing is also evidence of the strong impact of speech on the development of children's drawing.

We have had the opportunity of observing experimentally how children's drawing becomes real written language by giving them the task of symbolically depicting some more or less complex phrase. What was most clear in these experiments was a tendency on the part of school-age children to change from purely pictographic to ideographic writing, that is, to represent individual relations and meaning by abstract symbolic signs. We observed this dominance of speech over writing in one school child who wrote each word of the phrase in question as a separate drawing. For example, the phrase "I do not see the sheep, but they are there" was recorded as follows: a figure of a person ("I"), the same figure with its eyes covered ("don't see"), two sheep ("the sheep"), an index finger and several trees behind which the sheep can be seen ("but they are there"). The phrase "I respect you" was rendered as follows: a head ("I"), two human figures, one of which has his hat in hand ("respect") and another head ("you").

Thus, we see how the drawing obediently follows the phrase and how spoken language intrudes into children's drawings. In this process, the children frequently had to make genuine discoveries in inventing an appropriate mode of representation, and we were able to see that this is decisive in the development of writing and drawing in children.

SYMBOLISM IN WRITING

In connection with our general research, Luria undertook to create this moment of discovery of the symbolics of writing so as to be able to study it systematically.[6] In his experiments children who were as yet unable to write were confronted with the task of making some simple form of notation. The children were told to remember a certain number of phrases that greatly exceeded their natural memory capacity. When each child became convinced that he would not be able to remember them all, he was given a sheet of paper and asked to mark down or record the words presented in some fashion.

Frequently, the children were bewildered by this suggestion, saying that they could not write, but the experimenter furnished the child with a certain procedure and examined the extent to which the child was able to master it and extent to which the pencil-marks ceased to be simple playthings and became symbols for recalling the appropriate phrases. In the three-to-four-year-old stage, the child's notations are of no assistance in remembering the phrases; in recalling them, the child does not look at the paper. But we occasionally encountered some seemingly astonishing cases that were sharply at variance with this general observation. In these cases, the child also makes meaningless and undifferentiated squiggles and lines, but when he reproduces phrases it seems as though he is reading them; he refers to certain specific marks and can repeatedly indicate, without error, which marks denote which phrase. An entirely new relationship to these marks and a self-reinforcing motor activity arise: for the first time the marks become mnemo-technic symbols. For example, the children place individual marks on different parts of the page in such a way as to associate a certain phrase with each mark. A characteristic kind of topography arises—one mark in one corner means a cow, while another farther up means a chimney-sweep. Thus the marks are primitive indicatory signs for memory purposes.

We are fully justified in seeing the first precursor of future writing in this mnemotechnic stage. Children gradually transform these undifferentiated marks. Indicatory signs and symbolizing marks and scribbles are replaced by little figures and pictures, and these in turn give way to signs. Experiments have made it possible not only to describe the very moment of discovery itself but also to follow how the process occurs as a function of certain factors. For example, the content and forms introduced into the phrases in question first break down the meaningless nature of the notation. If we introduce quantity into the material, we can readily evoke a notation that reflects this quantity, even in four- and five-year-olds. (It was the need for recording quantity, perhaps, that historically first gave rise to writing.) In the same way, the introduction of color and form are conducive to the child's discovery of the principle of writing. For example, phrases such as "like black," "black smoke from a chimney," "there is white snow in winter," "a mouse with a long tail," or "Lyalya has two eyes and one nose" rapidly cause the child to change over from writing that functions as indicatory gesture to writing that contains the rudiments of representation.

It is easy to see that the written signs are entirely first-order symbols at this point, directly denoting objects or actions, and the child has yet to reach second-order symbolism, which involves the creation of written signs for the spoken symbols of words. For this the child must make a basic discovery—namely that one can draw not only things but also speech. It was only this discovery that led humanity to the brilliant method of writing by words and letters; the same thing leads children to letter writing. From the pedagogical point of view, this transition should be arranged by shifting the child's activity from drawing things to drawing speech. It is difficult to specify how this shift takes place, since the appropriate research has yet to lead to definite conclusions, and the generally accepted methods of teaching writing do not permit the observation of it. One thing only is certain—that the written language of children develops in this fashion, shifting from drawings of things to drawing of words. Various methods of teaching writing perform this in various ways. Many of them employ auxiliary gestures as a means of uniting the written and spoken symbol; others employ drawings that depict the appropriate objects. The entire secret of teaching written language is to prepare and organize this natural transition appropriately. As soon as it is achieved, the child has mastered the principle of written language and then it remains only to perfect this method.

Given the current state of psychological knowledge, our notion that make-believe play, drawing, and writing can be viewed as different moments in an essentially unified process of development of written language will appear to be very much overstated. The discontinuities and jumps from one mode of activity to another are too great for the relationship to seem evident. But experiments and psychological analysis lead us to this very conclusion. They show that, however complex the process of development of written language may seem, or however erratic, disjointed, and confused it may appear superficially, there is in fact a unified historical line that leads to the highest forms of written language. This higher form, which we will mention only in passing, involves the reversion of written language from second-order symbolism to first-order symbolism. As second-order symbols, written symbols function as designations for verbal ones. Understanding of written language is first effected through spoken language, but gradually this path is curtailed and spoken language disappears as the intermediate link. To judge from all the available evidence, written language becomes direct symbolism that is perceived in the same way as spoken language. We need only try to imagine the enormous changes in the cultural development of children that occur as a result of mastery of written language and the ability to read—and of thus becoming aware of everything that human genius has created in the realm of the written word.

PRACTICAL IMPLICATIONS

An overview of the entire developmental history of written language in children leads us naturally to three exceptionally important practical conclusions.

The first is that, from our point of view, it would be natural to transfer the teaching of writing to the preschool years. Indeed, if younger children are capable of discovering the symbolic function of writing, as Hetzer's experiments have shown, then the teaching of writing should be made the responsibility of preschool education. Indeed, we see a variety of circumstances which indicate that in the

Soviet Union the teaching of writing clearly comes too late from the psychological point of view. At the same time, we know that the teaching of reading and writing generally begins at age six in most European and American countries.

Hetzer's research indicates that eighty percent of three-year-olds can master an arbitrary combination of sign and meaning, while almost all six-year-olds are capable of this operation. On the basis of her observations, one may conclude that development between three and six involves not so much mastery of arbitrary signs as it involves progress in attention and memory. Therefore, Hetzer favors beginning to teach reading at earlier ages. To be sure, she disregards the fact that writing is second-order symbolism, whereas what she studied was first-order symbolism.

Burt reports that although compulsory schooling begins at age five in England, children between three and five are allowed into school if there is room and are taught the alphabet.[7] The great majority of children can read at four-and-a-half. Montessori is particularly in favor of teaching reading and writing at an earlier age.[8] In the course of game situations, generally through preparatory exercises, all the children in her kindergartens in Italy begin to write at four and can read as well as first-graders at age five.

But Montessori's example best shows that the situation is much more complex than it may appear at first glance. If we temporarily ignore the correctness and beauty of the letters her children draw and focus on the content of what they write, we find messages like the following: "Happy Easter to Engineer Talani and Headmistress Montessori. Best wishes to the director, the teacher, and to Doctor Montessori. Children's House, Via Campania," and so forth. We do not deny the possibility of teaching reading and writing to preschool children; we even regard it as desirable that a younger child enter school if he is able to read and write. But the teaching should be organized in such a way that reading and writing are necessary for something. If they are used only to write official greetings to the staff or whatever the teacher thinks up (and clearly suggests to them), then the exercise will be purely mechanical and may soon bore the child; his activity will not be manifest in his writing and his budding personality will not grow. Reading and writing must be something the child needs. Here we have the most vivid example of the basic contradiction that appears in the teaching of writing not only in Montessori's school but in most other schools as well, namely, that writing is taught as a motor skill and not as a complex cultural activity. Therefore, the issue of teaching writing in the preschool years necessarily entails a second requirement: writing must be "relevant to life"—in the same way that we require a "relevant" arithmetic.

A second conclusion, then, is that writing should be meaningful for children, that an intrinsic need should be aroused in them, and that writing should be incorporated into a task that is necessary and relevant for life. Only then can we be certain that it will develop not as a matter of hand and finger habits but as a really new and complex form of speech.

The third point that we are trying to advance as a practical conclusion is the requirement that writing be *taught* naturally. In this respect, Montessori has done a great deal. She has shown that the motor aspect of this activity can indeed be engaged in in the course of children's play, and that writing should be "cultivated" rather than "imposed." She offers a well-motivated approach to the development of writing.

Following this path, a child approaches writing as a natural moment in her development, and not as training from without. Montessori has shown that kindergarten is the appropriate setting for teaching reading and writing, and this means that the best method is one in which children do not learn to read and write but in which both these skills are found in play situations. For this it is necessary that letters become elements of children's life in the same way, for instance, that speech is. In the same way as children learn to speak, they should be able to learn to read and write. Natural methods of teaching reading and writing involve appropriate operations on the child's environment. Reading and writing should become necessary for her in her play. But what Montessori has done as regards the motor aspects of this skill should now be done in relation to the internal aspect of written language and its functional assimilation. Of course, it is also necessary to bring the child to an inner understanding of writing and to arrange that writing will be organized development rather than learning. For this we can indicate only an extremely general approach: in the same way that manual labor and mastery of line-drawing are preparatory exercises for Montessori in developing writing skills, drawing and play should be preparatory stages in the development of children's written language. Educators should organize all these actions and the entire complex process of transition from one mode of written language to another. They should follow it through its critical moments up to the discovery of the fact that one can draw not only objects but also speech. If we wished to summarize all these practical requirements and express them as a single one, we could say that children should be taught written language, not just the writing of letters.

The great basic idea that the world is not to be viewed as a complex of fully fashioned objects, but as a complex of processes, in which apparently stable objects, no less than the images of them inside our heads (our concepts), are undergoing incessant changes . . .

In the eyes of dialectical philosophy, nothing is established for all time, nothing is absolute or sacred. On everything and in everything it sees the stamp of inevitable decline; nothing can resist it save the unceasing process of formation and destruction, the unending ascent from lower to the higher—a process of which that philosophy itself is only a simple reflection within the thinking brain.

Friedrich Engels, Ludwig Feuerbach

Afterword

VERA JOHN-STEINER AND ELLEN SOUBERMAN

In this essay we hope to highlight several of Vygotsky's major theoretical assumptions, in particular those that could be the source of contemporary psychological research. After working for several years with the manuscripts and lectures that make up this volume, we came to recognize that Vygotsky's theory was primarily inductive, constructed midstream as he explored diverse phenomena such as memory, inner speech, and play. Our purpose is to explore in a systematic way those concepts that have had the greatest impact on us personally and intellectually while editing Vygotsky's manuscripts and preparing this work.

As readers, we discovered that the consequences of internalizing Vygotsky's ideas have a dynamic of their own. At first, an increasing familiarity with his ideas helps one go beyond the polarities of contemporary psychological writings; he offers a model for new psychological thought and research to those who are dissatisfied with the tension between traditional behaviorists and nativists. To some readers Vygotsky may seem to represent an intermediary position; but a careful reading reveals his emphasis on the complex transformations that constitute human growth, the understanding of which requires active participation on the part of the reader.

To Vygotsky, development was not merely a slow accumulation of unitary changes, but rather, as he wrote, "a complex dialectical process, characterized by periodicity, unevenness in the development of different functions, metamorphosis or qualitative transformation of one form into another, intertwining of external and internal factors, and adaptive processes" (chapter 5). And indeed, in this sense, his views of the history of the individual and the history of culture were similar. In both cases Vygotsky rejects the concept of linear development and incorporates into his conceptualization both evolutionary and revolutionary change. The recognition of these two interrelated forms of development is for him a necessary component of scientific thought.

Because it is not easy to conceptualize a dialectical process of change, we found that his concepts did not make their full impact until we attempted to combine our own research with his seminal ideas.[1] This process required working through, again and again, the expansion of his condensed but powerful concepts and applying them either to our work or to daily observations of human behavior. The cryptic nature of Vygotsky's writing, though it can be explained by the conditions of his life during his last years, forced us to search deeply for his most significant concepts. In this way we isolated those ideas that were strikingly original and which, forty years after his death, still offer new and unfulfilled promise for both psychology and education.

CONCEPTS OF DEVELOPMENT

Each chapter of this volume deals with some aspect of developmental change as Vygotsky conceived it. Although he is clearly committed to a theoretical position distinct from those of his influential contemporaries—Thorndike, Piaget, Koffka—he constantly returns to and analyzes their thinking in order to enrich and sharpen his own. While his contemporaries also addressed the issue of development, Vygotsky's approach differed from theirs in that he focused upon the historically shaped and culturally transmitted psychology of human beings. His analysis also differs from that of the early behaviorists. Vygotsky wrote:

> In spite of the significant advances attributable to behaviorist methodology, that method nevertheless is seriously limited. The psychologist's most vital challenge is that of uncovering and bringing to light the hidden mechanisms underlying complex human psychology. Though the behaviorist method is objective and adequate to the study of simple reflexive acts, it clearly fails when applied to the study of complex psychological processes. The inner mechanisms characteristic of these processes remain hidden.
>
> The naturalistic approach to behavior in general does not take into account the qualitative difference between human history and that of animals. The experimental ramification of this kind of analysis is that human behavior is studied without regard to the general history of human development.[2]

In contrast, Vygotsky emphasizes a theoretical approach, and consequently a methodology, that telescopes change. His effort in charting developmental change is, in part, to show the psychological implications of the fact that humans are active, vigorous participants in their own existence and that at each stage of development children acquire the means by which they can competently affect their world and themselves. Therefore, a crucial aspect of human mastery, beginning in infancy, is the creation and use of auxiliary or "artificial" stimuli; through such stimuli an immediate situation and the reaction linked to it are altered by active human intervention.

These auxiliary stimuli created by humans have no inherent relation to the existing situation; rather, humans introduce them as a means of active adaptation. Vygotsky views auxiliary stimuli as highly diverse: they include the tools of the culture into which the child is born, the language of those who relate to the child, and the ingenious means produced by the child himself, including the use of his own body. One of the most striking examples of this sort of tool use can be seen in the play activity of poor children who do not have access to prefabricated toys but who, nevertheless, are able to play house, train, and so on with whatever resources are available to them. Theoretical explorations of these activities in a developmental context are a recurrent theme of this volume, for Vygotsky sees play as the primary means of children's cultural development.

Piaget shares Vygotsky's emphasis upon an active organism. They share, as well, the ability to observe children astutely. However, Vygotsky's skills of observation were enhanced by his knowledge of dialectical materialism and his view of the human organism as highly plastic and of the environment as historically and culturally shifting contexts into which children are born and which they, too, will eventually change. While Piaget stresses biologically supported, universal stages of development, Vygotsky's emphasis is on the interaction between changing social conditions and the biological substrata of behavior. He wrote that "in order to study development in children, one must begin with an understanding of the dialectical unity of two principally different lines [the biological and the cultural], to adequately study this process, then, an experimenter must study both components and the laws which govern their *interlacement* at each stage of a child's development."[3]

Although the work of a great number of psychological theorists, including Piaget, has been characterized as interactionist, the premises of such an approach are still lacking full formulation. Some of the concepts described in this volume constitute the basis for a more fully articulated interactionist–dialectical analysis of development. One of the critical issues in any theory of development is the relation between the biological bases of behavior and the social conditions in and through which human activity takes place. A key concept Vygotsky proposed to represent this important interaction is the functional learning system. In the development of this notion he departed significantly both from the then-existing psychology and from concepts of learning strongly bound up with the study of animal behavior.

Vygotsky recognized, as had others before him, that functional systems are rooted in the most basic adaptive responses of the organism, such as unconditioned and conditioned reflexes. His theoretical contribution, however, is based on his description of the relation among these diverse processes:

> They are characterized by a new integration and co-relation of their parts. The whole and its parts develop parallel to each other and together. We shall call the first structures *elementary*; they are psychological wholes, conditioned chiefly by biological determinants. The latter structures which emerge in the process of cultural development are called *higher structures* . . . The initial stage is followed by that first structure's destruction, reconstruction, and transition to structures of the higher type. Unlike the direct, reactive processes, these latter structures are constructed on the basis of the use of signs and tools; these new formations unite both the direct and indirect means of adaptation.[4]

Vygotsky argued that in the course of development psychological systems arise which unite separate functions into new combinations and complexes. This concept was further elaborated by Luria, who states that the components and relations into which these unitary functions enter are formed during each individual's development and are dependent upon the social experiences of the child. The functional systems of an adult, then, are shaped essentially by her prior experiences as a child, the social aspects of which are more determinative than in traditional cognitive theory (including that of Piaget).

In this theory perhaps the most fundamental characteristic of developmental change is the manner in which previously separate and elementary functions are integrated into new functional learning systems: "Higher psychological functions are not superimposed as a second story over the elementary processes; they represent new psychological systems." These systems are changeable and are optimally adaptive to the particular tasks confronting the child as well as to the child's stage of development. Even though it may appear that children are learning in a purely external manner, that is, mastering new skills, the learning of any new operation is in fact the result of, and dependent on, a child's process of development. The formation of new functional learning systems includes a process akin to that of nourishment in body growth, wherein at any particular time certain nutrients are digested and assimilated while others are rejected.

An approach analogous to Vygotsky's has emerged from the contemporary discussions of the role of nutrition in development. Birch and Gussow, who conducted many cross-cultural studies of physical and intellectual growth, have advanced the following interactionist theory: "The effective environment of any organism is never merely the objective situation in which he finds himself, but is rather the product of an interaction between his unique organismic characteristics and whatever opportunities for experience his objective surroundings may provide."[5] In a similar vein, Vygotsky argues that because the historical conditions which determine to a large extent the opportunities for human experience are constantly changing, there can be no universal schema that adequately represents the dynamic relation between internal and external aspects of development. Therefore, a functional learning system of one child may not be identical to that of another, though there may be similarities at certain stages of development. Here, too, Vygotsky's analysis is different from that of Piaget, who describes universal stages that are identical for all children as a function of age.

This point of view, which aims at linking the biological substrata of development to the study of functions culturally and historically achieved, may be oversimplified and give rise to misunderstandings. Luria, Vygotsky's student and collaborator, sought to clarify the complex physiological implications of this view of the cognitive evolution of *Homo sapiens*:

> The fact that in the course of history man has developed new functions does not mean that each one relies on a new group of nerve cells and that new "centers" of higher nervous functions appear like those so eagerly sought by neurologists during the last third of the nineteenth century. The development of new "functional organs" occurs through the formation of *new functional systems*, which is a means for the unlimited development of cerebral activity. The human cerebral cortex, thanks to this principle, becomes an organ of civilization in which are hidden boundless possibilities, and does not require new morphological apparatuses every time history creates the need for a new function.[6]

The focus upon socially elaborated learning in Vygotsky's work emerges most clearly in his studies of mediated memory. It is in the course of interaction between children and adults that young learners identify effective means for remembering—means made accessible to them by those with more highly developed memory skills. The lack of recognition among educators of this social process, of the many ways in which an experienced learner can share his knowledge with a less advanced learner, limits the intellectual development of many students; their capabilities are viewed as biologically determined rather than socially facilitated. In addition to these studies of memory (chapter 3), Vygotsky explores the role of social and cultural experiences through an examination of children's play (chapter 7). In their play children both depend on and imaginatively transform those socially produced objects and forms of behavior made available to them in their particular environment. An ever-present theme in this volume is the Marxian concept of a historically determined human psychology. Some of Vygotsky's other writings, which are still unavailable in English, develop further his fundamental hypothesis that the higher mental functions are socially formed and culturally transmitted: "If one changes the tools of thinking available to a child, his mind will have a radically different structure."[7]

Through signs children are able to internalize the adaptive social means already available to them from society at large. For Vygotsky, one of the essential aspects of development is the increasing ability of children to control and direct their own behavior, a mastery made possible by the development of new psychological forms and functions and by the use of signs and tools in this process. At a later age children extend the boundaries of their understanding by integrating socially elaborated symbols (such as social values and beliefs, the cumulative knowledge of their culture, and the scientifically expanded concepts of reality) into their own consciousness.

In *Thought and Language* Vygotsky presents a sophisticated argument demonstrating that language, the very means by which reflection and elaboration of experience takes place, is a highly personal and at the same time a profoundly social human process. He sees the relation between the individual and the society as a dialectical process which, like a river and its tributaries, combines and separates the different elements of human life. They are never frozen polarities to him.

By far the most important sign-using behavior in children's development is human speech. Through speech children free themselves of many of the immediate constraints of their environment. They prepare themselves for future activity; they plan, order, and control their own behavior as well as that of others. Speech is also an excellent example of sign usage which, once internalized, becomes a pervasive and profound part of the higher psychological processes; speech acts to organize, unify, and integrate many disparate aspects of children's behavior, such as perception, memory, and problem solving (chapter 4).

He offers the contemporary reader a provocative avenue for dealing with a recurrent controversial issue, the relation between overt and covert processes.

Like words, tools and nonverbal signs provide learners with ways to become more efficient in their adaptive and problem-solving efforts. Vygotsky often illustrates the varied means of human adaptation with examples drawn from nonindustrialized societies:

> Counting fingers was once an important cultural triumph of humankind. It served as a bridge between immediate quantitative perception and counting. Thus, the Papuas of New Guinea began to count with the pinky of their left hand, follow through with the remaining left hand fingers, then add the left hand, forearm, elbow, shoulder, right shoulder, and so on, finishing with the pinky of the right hand. When this was insufficient they often used another person's fingers, or their own toes, or sticks, shells, and other small portable objects. In early counting systems, we may observe in developed and active form the same process that is present in rudimentary form during the development of a child's arithmetical reasoning.
>
> Similarly, the tying of knots as a reminder not to forget something is related to the psychology of everyday life. A person must remember something, to fulfill some request, do this or that, pick up some object. Not trusting his memory and unwilling to go by it, he often ties his hanky into a knot or uses a similar device, such as sticking a little piece of paper under the cover of his pocket watch. Later on, the knot is supposed to remind him of what he was supposed to do. And, this device often successfully carries out that function.
>
> Here, again, is an operation that is unthinkable and impossible in the case of animals. In the very fact of the introduction of an artificial, auxiliary means of memorizing, in the active creation and use of a stimulus as a tool for memory, we see a principally new and specifically human feature of behavior.[8]

The use of tools and signs share some important properties; both involve mediated activity. But they also diverge from each other: signs are internally oriented, according to Vygotsky, a means of psychological influence aimed at mastering oneself; tools, on the other hand, are externally oriented, aimed at mastering and triumphing over nature. The distinction between signs and tools is a good example of Vygotsky's analytical capacity to interweave diverse and similar aspects of human experience. Some other examples are thought and language, immediate and mediated memory, and, on a broader scale, the biological and the cultural, the individual and the social.

In a concise passage in which he describes a two-stage psychological transformation that captures the way in which the child internalizes her social experience, Vygotsky also depicts a dynamic that he believes is present throughout the entire span of a human life: "Every function in the child's cultural development appears twice, on two levels. First, on the social, and later on the psychological level; first, *between* people as an *interpsychological* category, and then inside the child, as an *intrapsychological* category. This applies equally to voluntary attention, to logical memory and to the formation of concepts. The actual relations between human individuals underlie all the higher functions" (chapter 4). In the buzzing confusion that surrounds the infant during the first few months of her life, parents assist her by pointing and carrying the child close to objects and places of adaptive significance (toys, refrigerator, cupboard, playpen), thus helping the child to ignore other irrelevant features of the environment (such adult objects as books, tools, and so on). This socially mediated attention develops into the child's more independent and voluntary attention, which she will come to use to classify her surroundings.

In contrast with the well-known formulation by J. B. Watson, who wrote of thought as "subvocal language," Vygotsky, in *Thought and Language*, describes how the growing child internalizes social language and makes it personal and how these two aspects of cognition, first independent of each other, are later joined: "Up to a certain point in time the two follow different lines, independently of each other . . . At a certain point these lines meet, whereupon thought becomes verbal and speech rational" (p. 44). In this way Vygotsky demonstrates the effectiveness of conceptualizing related functions not as an identity but as the unity of two diverse processes.

We believe this conception of human growth in its many varied manifestations is of value to contemporary psychological investigations. Though Vygotsky focused much of his research energies on the study of children, to view this great Russian psychologist as primarily a student of child development would be an error; he emphasized the study of development because he believed it to be the primary theoretical and methodological means necessary to unravel complex human processes, a view of human psychology that distinguishes him from his and our contemporaries. There was, for him, no real distinction between developmental psychology and basic psychological inquiry. Moreover, he recognized that an abstract theory is insuffiicent to capture the critical moments of change; and he demonstrated that the researcher must be an astute observer of children's play, their efforts at learning, their responses to teaching. The ingenuity of Vygotsky's experiments was a product of his skill and interest as both observer and experimenter.

EDUCATIONAL IMPLICATIONS

Throughout this volume Vygotsky explores the various temporal dimensions of human life. He never equates the historical development of humankind to the stages of individual growth, since he is opposed to the biogenetic theory of recapitulation. Rather, his concern is with the consequences of human activity as it transforms both nature and society. Although the labor of men and women to improve their world is rooted in the material conditions of their era, it is also affected by their capacity to learn from the past, to imagine, and to plan for the future. These specifically human abilities are absent in newborns, but by the age of three young children may already experience the tension between desires that can be fulfilled only in the future and demands for immediate gratification. Through play this contradiction is explored and temporarily resolved. And so Vygotsky places the beginnings of human imagination at the age of three: "Imagination is a new formation which is not present in the consciousness of the very young child, is totally absent in animals, and represents a specifically human form of conscious activity. Like all functions of consciousness, it originally arises from action. The old adage that child's play is imagination in action can be reversed: we can say that imagination in adolescents and schoolchildren is play without action" (chapter 7).

In their play children project themselves into the adult activities of their culture and rehearse their future roles and values. Thus, play is in advance of development, for in this manner children begin to acquire the motivation, skills, and attitudes necessary for their social participation, which can be fully achieved only with the assistance of their peers and elders.

During preschool and school years the conceptual abilities of children are stretched through play and the use of their imagination. In the course of their varied games they acquire and invent rules, or as Vygotsky describes it, "In play a child is always above his average age, above his daily behavior, in play it is as though he were a head taller than himself" (chapter 7). While imitating their elders in culturally patterned activities, children generate opportunities for intellectual development. Initially, their games are recollections and reenactments of real situations; but through the dynamics of their imagination and the recognition of implicit rules governing the activities they have reproduced in their games, children achieve an elementary mastery of abstract thought. In this sense, Vygotsky argued, play leads development.

Similarly, school instruction and learning is in advance of children's cognitive development. Vygotsky proposes a parallel between play and school instruction: both create a "zone of proximal development" (chapters 6 and 7), and in both contexts children elaborate socially available skills and knowledge that they will come to internalize. While in play all aspects of children's lives become themes in their games, in school both the content of what is being taught as well as the role of the specially trained adult who teaches them is carefully planned and more narrowly focused.

In an essay on the psychological ideas of L. S. Vygotsky, Leontiev and Luria summarize some of the specific features of classroom education:

> School education is qualitatively different from education in the broad sense. At school the child is faced with a particular task: to grasp the bases of scientific studies, i.e., a system of scientific conceptions.
>
> In the process of school education the child starts off from what have become his own complex generalizations and significances; but he does not so much proceed from them, as proceed onto a new path together with them, onto the path of intellectual analysis, comparison, unification, and establishment of logical relations. He reasons, following the explanations given to him and then reproducing new, for him, logical operations of transition from one generalization to other generalizations. The early concepts that have been built in the child in the process of living and which were assisted by rapport with his social environment (Vygotsky called them "everyday" or "spontaneous" concepts, spontaneous in the sense that they are formed aside from any process specially aimed at mastering them) are now switched to a new process, to a new specially cognitive relationship to the world, and so in this process the child's concepts are transformed and their structure changes. In the development of a child's consciousness the grasping of the bases of a science-system of concepts now takes the lead.[9]

In Vygotsky's lifetime he and Luria initiated studies aimed at examining the cognitive consequences of rapid social change and the specific impact of schooling.[10] In addition to his interest in cognitive development among nonliterate peoples, his concern encompassed other aspects of the social and educational transformations brought about by the October Revolution. These concerns occupy many contemporary educators in countries undergoing rapid modernization and urbanization. Even in the United States, where the concept of public education is two centuries old, similar issues arise because large groups of people have not yet been integrated into or benefited from mass education. Some of the issues of concern to Vygotsky that are still alive today are the length and scope of public education, the use of standardized tests to assess the educational potential of children, and effective models of teaching and curriculum.

Through the concept of the zone of proximal development as advanced by Vygotsky during intense educational debates in the 1930s, he telescopes, from the point of view of instruction, central tenets of his cognitive theory: the transformation of an interpersonal (social) process to an intrapersonal one; the stages of internalization; and the role of experienced learners. The zone of proximal development, he wrote, is "the distance between the [child's] actual developmental level as determined by independent problem solving and the level of potential development as determined through problem solving under adult guidance or in collaboration with more capable peers" (chapter 6).

Many educators, recognizing that the rate of learning may vary from child to child, isolate particularly "slow learners" from their teachers as well as their peers through the use of programmed and frequently mechanized instruction. In contrast, Vygotsky, because he views learning as a profoundly social process, emphasizes dialogue and the varied roles that language plays in instruction and in mediated cognitive growth. The mere exposure of students to new materials through oral lectures neither allows for adult guidance nor for collaboration with peers. To implement the concept of the zone of proximal development in instruction, psychologists and educators must collaborate in the analysis of the internal ("subterranean") developmental processes which are stimulated by teaching and which are needed for subsequent learning. In this theory, then, teaching represents the means through which development is advanced; that is, the socially elaborated contents of human knowledge and the cognitive strategies necessary for their internalization are evoked in the learners according to their "actual developmental levels." Vygotsky criticizes educational intervention that lags behind developed psychological processes instead of focusing upon emerging functions and capabilities. A particularly imaginative application of these principles are Paolo Freire's literacy campaigns in Third World countries. Because he adapted his educational methods to the specific historical and cultural setting in which his students lived, they were able to combine their "spontaneous" concepts (those based on social practice) with those introduced by teachers in instructional settings.[11]

VYGOTSKY'S HISTORICAL–CULTURAL APPROACH

Perhaps the most distinguishing theme of Vygotsky's writings is his emphasis on the unique qualities of our species, how as human beings we actively realize and change ourselves in the varied contexts of culture and history. Repeatedly in this volume Vygotsky differentiates the adaptive capabilities of animals from those of humans. The critical factor on which this distinction is based is the historically created and culturally elaborated dimensions of human life that are absent from the social organization of animals. In the development of higher functions—that is, in the internalization of the processes of knowing—the particulars of human social existence are reflected in human cognition: an individual has the capacity to externalize and share with other members of her social group her understanding of their shared experience.

The relative immaturity of the human infant, in contrast with other species, necessitates a lengthy reliance on caretaking adults, a circumstance that creates a basic psychological contradiction for the infant: on the one hand he is totally dependent on organisms vastly more experienced than himself, and on the other hand he reaps the benefits of a socially developed and optimal setting for learning. Although children are dependent on lengthy nurturance and caretaking, they are active participants in their own learning within the supportive contexts of family and community. As Edward E. Berg pointed out:

> Just as the tools of labor change historically, so the tools of thinking change historically. And just as new tools of labor give rise to new social structures, new tools of thinking give rise to new mental structures. Traditionally, it was thought that such things as the family and the state always existed in more or less their present form. Likewise, one also tends to view the structure of the mind as something universal and eternal. To Vygotsky, however, both social structures and mental structures turn out to have very definite historical roots, and are quite specific products of certain levels of tool development.[12]

Vygotsky's study of human development was deeply influenced by Friedrich Engels, who stressed the critical role of labor and tools in transforming the relation between human beings and their environment. The role of tools in human development was described by Engels as follows: "The tool specifically symbolizes human activity, man's transformation of nature: production."[13] Such an approach requires an understanding of the active role of history in human psychological development. In *The Dialectics of Nature* Engels presented some key concepts that were elaborated by Vygotsky. They both criticized psychologists and philosophers who held the view "that only nature affects man and only natural conditions determine man's historic development," and emphasized that in the course of history man, too, "affects nature, changes it, creates for himself new natural conditions of existence."[14] Furthermore, Vygotsky argued that the effect of tool use upon humans is fundamental not only because it has helped them relate more effectively to their external environment but also because tool use has had important effects upon internal and functional relationships within the human brain.

Although Engels and Vygotsky based their theories on the limited archaeological findings available to them during the years in which they wrote, contemporary archaeologists and physical anthropologists such as the Leakeys and Sherwood Washburn have interpreted more recent findings in a manner consistent with Engels' and Vygotsky's point of view. Washburn states, "It was the success of the simplest tools that started the whole trend of human evolution and led to the civilization of today." Most likely Vygotsky would have agreed with Washburn, who views the evolution of human life from our primate ancestors as resulting in "intelligent, exploratory, playful, and vigorous primates . . . and that tools, hunting, fire, complex social speech, the human way and the brain evolved together to produce ancient man."[15] These archaeological discoveries support Vygotsky's concepts of what it is to be human.

The impact of Vygotsky's work—as that of great theoreticians everywhere—is both general and specific. Cognitive psychologists as well as educators are interested in exploring the present-day implications of his notions, whether they refer to play, to the genesis of scientific concepts, or to the relation of language and thought. The men and women who were his students forty years ago still debate his ideas with the intensity and vigor due a contemporary—and we who worked as his editors found many possible, sometimes contradictory, interpretations of his work. But there is a powerful thread drawing together Vygotsky's diverse and stimulating writings: it is the way in which his mind worked. His legacy in an increasingly destructive and alienating world is to offer through his theoretical formulations a powerful tool for restructuring human life with an aim toward survival.[16]

Notes

INTRODUCTION

1. K. N. Kornilov, "Psychology and Marxism," in K. N. Kornilov, ed., *Psychology and Marxism* (Leningrad: State Publishing House, 1925), pp. 9–24. L. S. Vygotsky, "Consciousness as a Problem in the Psychology of Behavior," in Kornilov, ed., *Psychology and Marxism*, pp. 175–198. See also K. N. Kornilov, "Psychology in the Light of Dialectical Materialism," in C. Murchison, ed., *Psychologies of 1930* (Worcester: Clark University Press, 1930; rpt., New York: Arno Press, 1973).

2. Friedrich Engels, *Dialectics of Nature* (New York: International Publishers, 1940), p. 40.

3. P. P. Blonsky, *Studies in Scientific Psychology* (Moscow: State Publishing House, 1911).

4. R. Thurnwald, "Psychologie des primitiven Menschen," in *Handbuch der vergleichenden Psychologie* (Munich, 1922). L. Levy-Bruhl, *Primitive Mentality* (New York: Macmillan, 1923).

5. A. R. Luria, *Cognitive Development: Its Cultural and Social Foundations* (Cambridge: Harvard University Press, 1976).

6. Z. M. Istomina, "The Development of Voluntary Memory in Preschool Age Children," *Soviet Psychology*, 13, no. 4 (1975): 5-64.

7. M. Cole and I. Maltzman, eds., *A Handbook of Contemporary Soviet Psychology* (New York: Basic Books, 1969). A. V. Zaporozhets and D. B. Elkonin, eds., *The Psychology of Preschool Children* (Cambridge: MIT Press, 1971).

CHAPTER 1

1. K. Stumpf, "Zur Methodik der Kinderpsychologie," *Zeitsch. f. pädag. Psychol.*, 2 (1900).

2. A. Gesell, *The Mental Growth of the Preschool Child* (New York: Macmillan, 1925; Russian ed., Moscow-Leningrad: Gosizdat., 1930).

3. W. Köhler, *The Mentality of Apes* (New York: Harcourt, Brace, 1925).

4. K. Buhler, *The Mental Development of the Child* (New York: Harcourt, Brace, 1930; Russion ed., 1924).

5. This particular experiment was described by D. E. Berlyne, "Children's Reasoning and Thinking," in *Carmichael's Manual of Child Psychology*, 3rd ed., Paul H. Mussen, ed. (New York: John Wiley, 1970), pp. 939–981.

6. C. Buhler, *The First Year of Life* (New York: Day, 1930).

7. K. Buhler, *Mental Development*, pp. 49–51. See also C. Buhler, *First Year*. The linguistic capabilities of chimpanzees are currently the subject of controversy among psychologists and linguists. It seems clear that chimpanzees are capable of more complex signing than expected at the time Buhler and Vygotsky wrote these passages. However, the inferences about cognitive and linguistic competence warranted by these observations are still hotly debated.

8. S. A. Shapiro and E. D. Gerke, described in M. Ya. Basov, *Fundamentals of General Pedology* (Moscow-Leningrad: Gosizdat., 1928).

9. P. Guillaume and I. Meyerson, "Recherches sur l'usage de l'instrument chez les singes," *Journal de Psychologie*, 27 (1930): 177–236.

10. Research on aphasia was barely begun by Vygotsky during his own lifetime. The error of this conclusion and subsequent changes in his theory regarding aphasia may be found in the work of A. R. Luria; see *Traumatic Aphasia* (The Hague: Mouton, 1970).

11. W. Stern, *Psychology of Early Childhood up to the Sixth Year of Age* (New York: Holt, Rinehart and Winston, 1924; Russian ed., Petrograd, 1915).

12. J. Piaget, *The Language and Thought of the Child* (New York: Meridian Books, 1955; also International Library of Psychology, 1925). The differences between Vygotsky's and Piaget's views of early language development and the role of egocentric speech is treated extensively in chapter 3 of Vygotsky's *Thought and Language* (Cambridge: MIT Press, 1962) and in Piaget's volume of essays, *Six Psychological Studies* (New York: Random House, 1967).

13. See R. E. Levina, for L. S. Vygotsky's ideas on the planning role of speech in children, *Voprosi Psikhologii*, 14 (1938): 105–115. Although Levina made these observations in the late 1920s, they remain unpublished except for this brief explication.

14. Piaget, *Language and Thought*, p. 110.

15. A fuller description of these experiments is presented in chapter 7 of *Thought and Language*.

CHAPTER 2

1. A. Binet, "Perception de'enfants," *Revue Philosophique*, 30 (1890): 582–611. Stern, *Psychology of Early Childhood*.

2. A. A. Potebnya, *Thought and Language* (Kharkhov, 1892), p. 6.

3. K. Koffka, *The Growth of the Mind* (London: Routledge and Kegan Paul, 1924).

4. R. Lindner, *Gas Taubstumme Kind in Vergleich mit vollstandigen Kinder* (Leipzig, 1925).

5. K. Lewin, *Wille, Vorsatz und Beduerfniss* (Berlin: Springer, 1926).

CHAPTER 3

1. E. R. Jaensch, *Eidetic Imagery* (New York: Harcourt, Brace, 1930).

2. Vygotsky is referring here to the technique of using knotted rope as a mnemonic device among Peruvian Indians. No reference is given in the text, but from other manuscripts it appears that the writing of E. B. Taylor and Levy-Bruhl provided these examples.

3. These observations are taken from an article by A. N. Leontiev, "Studies on the Cultural Development of the Child," *Journal of Genetic Psychology*, 40 (1932): 52–83.

4. A fuller description of this technique may be found in A. R. Luria, "The Development of Mental Functions in Twins," *Character and Personality*, 5 (1937): 35–47.

5. L. V. Zankov, *Memory* (Moscow: Uchpedgiz., 1949).

6. A. N. Leontiev, "The Development of Mediated Memory," *Problemi Defektologiga*, no. 4 (1928).

7. See H. Werner, *Comparative Psychology of Mental Development* (New York: Science Editions, 1961), pp. 216ff.

8. See Vygotsky, *Thought and Language*, chapter 6, for a more extensive discussion of the distinction.

CHAPTER 4

1. G. Hegel, "Encyklopadie, Erster Theil. Die Logik" (Berlin, 1840), p. 382, cited in K. Marx, *Capital* (Modern Library Edition, 1936).

2. Marx, *Capital*, p. 199.

CHAPTER 5

1. Engels, *Dialectics of Nature*, p. 172.

2. H. Werner, *The Comparative Psychology of Mental Development* (New York: International Universities Press, 1948).

3. K. Lewin, *A Dynamic Theory of Personality* (New York: McGraw-Hill, 1935).

4. Stern, *Psychology of Early Childhood*.

5. Exact references are not included, but in his other writings, Vygotsky quotes extensively from *Capital*, vol. 1.

6. E. Titchener, *Textbook of Psychology* (Moscow, 1914, in Russian).

7. P. P. Blonsky, *Essays in Scientific Psychology* (Moscow: State Publishing House, 1921).

8. For an extended discussion of the importance of reaction time experiments in early twentieth-century psychology, see E. G. Boring, "The Psychology of Controversy," *Psychological Review*, 36 (1929): 97–121.

9. Several of Cattell's papers on the reaction time study are reprinted in W. Dennis, *Readings in the History of Psychology* (New York: Appleton-Century-Crofts, 1948).

10. N. Ach *Über die Willenstatigkeit und das Denken* (1905).

11. For an outstanding application of these ideas to the development of voluntary memory in preschool age children, see the article by Istomina in *Soviet Psychology*, 12, no. 4 (1975): 5–64.

CHAPTER 6

1. Piaget, *Language and Thought*.

2. William James, *Talks to Teachers* (New York: Norton, 1958), pp. 36–37.

3. Koffka, *Growth of the Mind*.

4. E. L. Thorndike, *The Psychology of Learning* (New York: Teachers College Press, 1914).

5. Dorothea McCarthy, *The Language Development of the Pre-school Child* (Minneapolis: University of Minnesota Press, 1930).

6. Köhler, *Mentality of Apes*.

7. Piaget, *Language and Thought*.

CHAPTER 7

1. J. Sully, *Studies of Childhood* (Moscow, 1904, in Russian), p. 48.

2. Lewin, *Dynamic Theory of Personality*, p. 96.

3. See K. Goldstein, *Language and Language Disorders* (New York: Greene and Stratton, 1948).

4. Koffka, *Growth of the Mind*, pp. 381ff.

CHAPTER 8

1. J. M. Baldwin, *Mental Development in the Child and the Race* (New York, 1895; Russian ed., 1912).

2. Wurth (reference not available).

3. H. Hetzer, *Die Symbolische Darstelling in der fruhen Windhert*, (Vienna: Deutscher Verlag für Jugend und Volk, 1926), p. 92.

4. K. Buhler, *Mental Development of the Child*.

5. J. Sully, *Studies of Childhood* (London, 1895).

6. A. R. Luria, "Materials on the Development of Writing in Children," *Problemi Marksistkogo Vospitaniya*, I (1929): 143–176.

7. C. Burt, *Distribution of Educational Abilities* (London: P. S. King and Sons, 1917).

8. M. Montessori, *Spontaneous Activity in Education* (New York: Schocken, 1965).

AFTERWORD

1. See Nan Elsasser and Vera John-Steiner, "An Interactionist Approach to Advancing Literacy," *Harvard Educational Review*, 47, no. 3 (August 1977): 355–370.

2. Translation of passage from "Tool and Symbol" and *Development of Higher Psychological Functions* not included in this text. Vygotsky used the term "natural" widely; see pp. 38–39, above.

3. In this volume, the editors have interpreted Vygotsky's use of "natural" aspects of behavior to mean biologically given features, such as reflexes present at birth. An additional interpretation of "natural" can be gained from the following passage taken from A. N. Leontiev's, A. R. Luria's, and B. M. Teplov's preface to Vygotsky's *Development of Higher Psychological Functions.*

> His attempt to show that it was impossible to reduce the formation of man's higher mental functions to the process of the development of their elementary forms leads to the false division at the genetic plane and at the plane of coexistence at higher levels of development. Thus, for example, memory development is presented as going through two stages: the stage of purely natural memory which terminates at a preschool age and the following stage of development of a higher, mediated memory. The development of co-existing forms of memory is treated in the same way. One form rests exclusively on biological foundations, and others are the product of the child's social and cultural development. This opposition which appears in L. S. Vygotsky's writings and in the research of his collaborators justifiably was criticized in its time. It is truly without foundation: after all, even in very young children psychological processes are formed under the influence of verbal interaction with adults and consequently are not "natural." The young child's memory processes are not "natural" because they already have changed as a result of language acquisition. We can say the same with regard to cases of the preservation of a sharply distinguished "natural" eidetic memory which turns out to be subject to transformation in man.

While pointing out the inadequacy of Vygotsky's false contrast between natural (organic) and higher (cultural) forms of mental processes, we must emphasize that this contrast in no way is implied from his general theoretical position.

Although Vygotsky has been criticized for posing this artificial duality between the natural and the cultural, as Leontiev and Luria point out, the distinction is in fact an abstraction, a vehicle for describing a very complex process. "The child's mental development is a continuous process of gaining active control over initially passive mental functions. To gain this control the child learns to use signs and thus converts these 'natural' mental functions into sign-mediated, cultural functions." Edward E. Berg, "L. S. Vygotsky's Theory of the Social and Historical Origins of Consciousness" (Ph.D. Diss., University of Wisconsin, 1970), p. 164.

4. This passage is from the unedited translation of "Tool and Symbol."

5. Herbert G. Birch and Joan Dye Gussow, *Disadvantaged Children: Health, Nutrition and School Failure* (New York: Harcourt, Brace and World, 1970), p. 7.

6. A. R. Luria, "L. S. Vygotsky and the Problem of Functional Localization," *Soviet Psychology,* 5, no. 3 (1967): 53–57.

7. E. Berg, "Vygotsky's Theory," p. 46.

8. Translation of passage from *Development of Higher Psychological Functions* not included in text.

9. A. N. Leontiev and A. R. Luria, "The Psychological Ideas of L. S. Vygotskii," in B. B. Wolman, ed., *Historical Roots of Contemporary Psychology* (New York: Harper and Row, 1968), pp. 338–367.

10. A. R. Luria, *Cognitive Development: Its Cultural and Social Foundations* (Cambridge: Harvard University Press, 1976).

11. P. Freire, *Pedagogy of the Oppressed* (New York: Seabury, 1970).

12. "Vygotsky's Theory," pp. 45–46.

13. K. Marx and F. Engels, *Selected Works* (Moscow: 1953), p. 63.

14. Engels, *Dialectics of Nature* (New York: International Publishers, 1940), p. 172.

15. "Tools and Human Evolution," *Scientific American*, 203, no. 3 (1960): 63–75.

16. We would especially like to thank Stan Steiner and Ricardo Maez for their continued support through our many years of work on this volume and for their recognition of the importance of Vygotsky's writings to our joint futures.

Vygotsky's Works

IN RUSSIAN

1915

"The Tragedy of Hamlet, Prince of Denmark." Private archives of L. S. Vygotsky. Manuscript.

1916

"Literary Remarks on *Petersburg* by Andrey Beliy." *The New Way,* 1916, no. 47, pp. 27–32.

Review of *Petersburg* by Andrey Beliy. *Chronicle,* 1916, no. 12, pp. 327–328.

Review of *Furrows and Bounds* by Vyacheslav Ivanov published in (*Musatet,* 1916). *Chronicle,* 1916, no. 10, pp. 351–352.

"The Tragedy of Hamlet, Prince of Denmark." Private archives of L. S. Vygotsky. Manuscript.

1917

Review of *Joy Will Be* (a play) by D. Merezhkovsky (published in *The Lights,* 1916). *Chronicle,* 1917, no. 1, pp. 309–310.

Foreword to and remarks on "The Priest" (a poem) by N. L. Brodsky. *Chronicle,* 1917, nos. 5–6, pp. 366–367.

1922

"About the Methods of Teaching Literature in Secondary Schools."
Report on the District Scientific Methodological Conference, Aug. 7, 1922. Private archives of L. S. Vygotsky. Manuscript, 17 pp.

1923

"The Investigation of the Processes of Language Comprehension Using Multiple Translation of Text from One Language to Another." Private archives of L. S. Vygotsky. Manuscript, 8 pp.

1924

Vygotsky, L. S., ed. *Problems of Education of Blind, Deaf-Dumb and Retarded Children.* Moscow: SPON NKP Publishing House, 1924.

"Methods of Reflexological and Psychological Investigation." Report of the National Meeting of Psychoneurology, Leningrad, Jan. 2, 1924. In *The Problems of Contemporary Psychology*, II, 26–46. Leningrad: Government Publishing House, 1926.

"Psychology and Education of Defective Children." In *Problems of Education of Blind, Deaf-Dumb and Retarded Children*, pp. 5–30. Moscow: SPON NKP Publishing House, 1924.

Foreword to *Problems of Education of Blind, Deaf-Dumb and Retarded Children.* Moscow: SPON NKP Publishing House, 1924.

"The Principles of Education of Physically Defective Children." Report of the Second Meeting of SPON, Dec. 1924. *Public Education*, 1925, no. 1, pp. 112–120.

1925

Review of *The Auxiliary School* by A. N. Graborov. *Public Education*, 1925, no. 9, pp. 170–171.

Foreword to *Beyond the Pleasure Principle* by S. Freud. Moscow: Contemporary Problems, 1925. (With A. R. Luria.)

Foreword to *General and Experimental Psychology* by A. F. Lasursky. Leningrad: Government Publishing House, 1925.

"The Principles of Social Education of Deaf-Dumb Children." Private archives of L. S. Vygotsky. Manuscript, 26 pp.

The Psychology of Art. Moscow: Moscow Art Publishing House, 1965 (379 pp.); 2nd ed., 1968 (576 pp.).

"The Conscious as a Problem of the Psychology of Behavior." In *Psychology and Marxism*, I, 175–198. Moscow-Leningrad: Government Publishing House, 1925.

1926–1927

Graphics of Bikhovsky. Moscow: Contemporary Russia Publishing House, 1926.

"Methods of Teaching Psychology." (Course program.) The State Archives of Moscow District, fol. 948, vol. I, set 613, p. 25.

"About the Influence of Speech Rhythm on Breathing." In *Problems of Contemporary Psychology*, II, 169–173. Leningrad: Government Publishing House, 1926.

Pedagogical Psychology. Moscow: The Worker of Education Publishing House, 1926.

"Introspection" by Koffka. In *Problems of Contemporary Psychology*, pp. 176–178. Moscow-Leningrad: Government Publishing House, 1926.

Foreword to *Principles of Learning Based upon Psychology* by E. L. Thorndike (tr. from the English), pp. 5–23. Moscow: The Worker of Education Publishing House, 1926.

Foreword to *The Practice of Experimental Psychology, Education and Psychotechnics* by R. Schulz (tr. from the German), pp. 3–5. Moscow: Problems of Labor Publishing House, 1926. (With A. R. Luria.)

"The Problem of Dominant Reactions." In *Problems of Contemporary Psychology*, II, 100–123. Leningrad: Government Publishing House, 1926.

Review of *The Psyche of Proletarian Children* by Otto Rulle (Moscow-Leningrad, 1926). Private archives of L. S. Vygotsky. Manuscript, 3 pp.

"The Biogenetic Law in Psychology and Education." *The Great Soviet Encyclopedia*, 1927, vol. VI, cols. 275–279.

"Defect and Supercompensation." In *Retradation, Blindness and Mutism*, pp. 51–76. Moscow: Down with Illiteracy Publishing House, 1927.

"The Historical Meaning of the Crisis in Psychology." Private archives of L. S. Vygotsky. Manuscript, 430 pp.

The Manual of Experimental Psychology. Moscow: Government Publishing House, 1927. (With V. A. Artomov, N. A. Bernshtein, N. F. Dobrinin, and A. R. Luria.)

Readings in Psychology. Moscow-Leningrad: Government Publishing House, 1927. (With V. A. Artomov, N. F. Dobrinin, and A. R. Luria.)

Review of *The Method of Psychological Observation of Children* by M. Y. Basov (Moscow-Leningrad: Government Publishing House, 1926). *Teacher of the People*, 1927, no. 1, p. 152.

"Contemporary Psychology and Art." *Soviet Art*, 1927, no. 8, pp. 5–8; 1928, no. 1, pp. 5–7.

1928

"Anomalies of Cultural Development of the Child." Report to the Department of Defectology, Institute of Education of the Second Moscow State University, April 28, 1928. *Problems of Defectology*, 1929, no. 2 (8), pp. 106–107.

"Behaviorism." *The Great Soviet Encyclopedia*, 1928, vol. III, cols. 483–486.

"Sick Children." *Pedagogical Encyclopedia*, 1928, vol. II, cols. 396–397.

"The Will and Its Disturbances." *The Great Soviet Encyclopedia*, 1928, vol. V, cols. 590–600.

"The Education of Blind-Deaf-Mute Children." *Pedagogical Encyclopedia*, 1928, vol. II, cols. 395–396.

"Report of the Conference of Methods of Psychology Teaching in Teachers' College," April 10, 1928. The State Archives of Moscow District, fol. 948, vol. I, pp. 13–15.

"The Genesis of Cultural Forms of Behavior." Lecture, Dec. 7, 1928. Private archives of L. S. Vygotsky. Stenography, 28 pp.

"Defect and Compensation." *Pedagogical Encyclopaedia*, 1928, vol. II, cols. 391–392.

"The Instrumental Method in Psychology." In *The Main Problems of Pedology in the USSR*, pp. 158–159. Moscow, 1928.

"The Results of a Meeting." *Public Education*, 1928, no. 2, pp. 56–67.

"Invalids." *Pedagogical Encyclopaedia*, 1928, vol. II, col. 396.

"The Question of the Dynamics of Children's Character. In *Pedology and Education*, pp. 99–119. Moscow: The Worker of Education Publishing House, 1928.

"The Question Concerning the Duration of Childhood in the Retarded Child." Report to the Meeting of Defectology Department by the Institute of Pedagogics of the Second Moscow State University, Dec. 18, 1928. *Problems of Defectology,* 1929, no. 2(8), p. 111.

"The Question of Multilingualism in Childhood." Private archives of L. S. Vygotsky. Manuscript, 32 pp.

"Lectures on the Psychology of Development." Private archives of L. S. Vygotsky. Stenography, 54 pp.

"The Methods of Investigating Retarded Children." Report to the First National Conference of Auxiliary School Workers. Archives of the Institute of Defectology, Academy of Pedagogical Sciences, USSR. Manuscript, 1 p.

"On the Intersections of Soviet and Foreign Education." *Problems of Defectology,* 1928, no. 1, pp. 18–26.

"To the Memory of V. M. Bekhterev." *Public Education,* 1928, no. 2, pp. 68–70.

The Pedology of School-age Children. Lectures 1–8. Moscow: Extension Division of the Second Moscow State University, 1928.

"The Problem of the Cultural Development of Children." *Pedology,* 1928, no. 1, pp. 58–77.

"Psychological Science in the USSR." In *The Social Sciences of the USSR (1917–1927),* pp. 25–46. Moscow: The Worker of Education Publishing House, 1928.

"The Psychological Basis for Teaching Dumb-Mute Children." *Pedagogical Encyclopaedia,* 1928, vol. II, col. 395.

"The Psychological Basis for Teaching Blind Children." *Pedagogical Encyclopaedia,* 1928, vol. II, cols. 394–395.

"Psychophysiological Basis for Teaching Abnormal Children." *Pedagogical Encyclopaedia,* 1928, vol. II, cols. 392–393.

"The Investigation of the Development of the Difficult Child." In *Leading Problems of Pedology in the USSR,* pp. 132–136. Moscow, 1928.

"Abnormal and Normal Children." *Pedagogical Encyclopaedia,* 1928, vol. II, col. 398.

"The Sociopsychological Basis for Teaching the Abnormal Child." *Pedagogical Encyclopaedia,* 1928, vol. II, cols. 393–394.

"The Three Main Types of Abnormality." *Pedagogical Encyclopaedia,* 1928, vol. II, col. 392.

"Difficult Childhood." Lectures 3 and 4. Archives of the Institute of Defectology, Academy of Pedagogical Sciences, USSR. Stenography, 9 pp.

"The Retarded Child." *Pedagogical Encyclopaedia,* 1928, vol. II, cols. 397–398.

1929

"Lectures on Abnormal Childhood." *Problems of Defectology,* 1929 (1930), no. 2 (8), pp. 108–112.

"Developmental Roots of Thinking and Speech." *Natural Science and Marxism,* 1929, no. 1, pp. 106–133.

"Genius." *The Great Soviet Encyclopedia,* 1929, vol. VI, cols. 612–613.

"About the Plan of Research Work for the Pedology of National Minorities." *Pedology,* 1929, no. 3, pp. 367–377.

"The Intellect of Anthropoids in the Work of W. Köhler." *Natural Science and Marxism,* 1929, no. 2, pp. 131–153.

"Some Methodological Questions." The Archives of the Academy of Pedagogical Science, USSR, fol. 4, vol. I, no. 103, pp. 51–52, 73–74.

"The Main Postulates of the Plan for Pedagogical Research Work Concerning Difficult Children." *Pedology,* 1929, no. 3, pp. 333–342.

"The Main Problems of Contemporary Defectology." Report to the Defectological Section of the Institute of Education, Moscow State University. In *The Works of the Second Moscow State University,* I, 77-106. Moscow, 1929.

"History of the Cultural Development of the Normal and Abnormal Child." Private archives of L. S. Vygotsky. 1929–1930. Manuscript.

The Pedology of Teenagers. Lectures 1–4, 5–8. Moscow: Extension Division of the Second Moscow State University, 1929.

Subject and Methods of Contemporary Psychology. Moscow: Extension Division of the Second Moscow State University, 1929.

"The Problem of Cultural Age." Lecture, Feb. 15, 1929. Private archives of L. S. Vygotsky. Stenography, 18 pp.

"The Development of Active Attention during Childhood." In *Problems of Marxist Education,* I, 112–142. Moscow: Academy of Communist Education, 1929. Also in *Selected Psychological Investigations,* pp. 389–426. Moscow: Academy of Pedagogical Sciences Publishing House, 1956.

Review of *School Dramatic Work as the Basis for Investigation of the Child's Creativity* by Dimitrieva, Oldenburg, and Perekrestova (Moscow: Government Publishing House, 1929). *Art in the School,* 1929, no. 8, pp. 29–31.

Review of *Contemporary Advances in Animal Psychology* by D. N. Kashkarov (Moscow: Government Publishing House, 1928). *Natural Science and Marxism,* 1929, no. 2, pp. 209–211.

Review of *The Language of Children* by C. Stern and W. Stern (Leipzig: Barth, 1928). *Natural Science and Marxism,* 1929, no. 3, pp. 185–192.

Review of *Means of Educational Influence* by S. M. Rives (Moscow: The Worker of Education Publishing House, 1929). *Pedology,* 1929, no. 4, pp. 645–646.

"The Structure of Interests in Adolescence and the Interests of the Teenage Worker. In *Problems of Pedology of the Teenage Worker,* IV, pp. 25–68. Moscow, 1929.

1930

"The Biological Base of Affect." *I Want to Know Everything,* 1930, nos. 15–16, pp. 480–481.

Foreword to materials collected by workers of the Institute of Scientific Education, April 13, 1930. Archives of the Academy of Pedagogical Sciences, USSR, fol. 4, vol. I, no. 103, pp. 81–82.

"Is It Possible to Simulate Extraordinary Memory?" *I Want to Know Everything,* 1930, no. 24, pp. 700–703.

"Imagination and Creativity in Childhood." Private archives of L. S. Vygotsky. Manuscript.

Problems of Defectology, VI. L. S. Vygotsky, ed. 1930. (With D. I. Asbukhin and L. V. Zankov.)

Foreword to *The Essay of Spiritual Development of the Child* by K. Buhler. Moscow: The Worker of Education Publishing House, 1930.

"Extraordinary Memory." *I Want to Know Everything*, 1930, no. 19, pp. 553–554.

"The Instrumental Method in Psychology." Report in the Academy of Communist Education. Private archives of L. S. Vygotsky. Manuscript.

"The Question of Speech Development and Education of the Deaf-Mute Child. Report to the Second National Conference of School Workers. Archives of the Institute of Defectology, Academy of Pedagogical Sciences, USSR. Manuscript, 2 pp.

"The Problem of the Development of Interests in Adolescence." *Education of Workers*, 1930, nos. 7–8, pp. 63–81.

"The Cultural Development of Abnormal and Retarded Children." Report to the First Meeting for Investigation of Human Behavior, Moscow, Feb. 1, 1930. In *Psychological Sciences in the USSR*, pp. 195–196. Moscow-Leningrad: Medgiz, 1930.

"New Developments in Psychological Research." Report to the Third National Meeting of Child Care, May 1930. *The Internat*, 1930, no. 7, pp. 22–27.

"Psychological Systems." Report to the Neurology Clinic of the First Moscow State University, Oct. 9, 1930. Private archives of L. S. Vygotsky. Stenography.

"Tool and Sign." Private archives of L. S. Vygotsky. Manuscript.

"The Connection between Labor Activity and the Intellectual Development of the Child." *Pedology*, 1930, nos. 5–6, pp. 588–596.

"The Behavior of Man and Animals." Private archives of L. S. Vygotsky, 1929–1930. Manuscript.

Foreword to *Teachers' Guide to the Investigation of the Educational Process* by B. R. Bekingem. Moscow: The Worker of Education Publishing House, 1930.

Foreword to *Investigation of the Intellect of Anthropoids* by W. Köhler. Moscow: Publishing House of the Communist Academy, 1930.

"The Problem of the Higher Intellectual Functions in the System of Psychological Investigation." *Psychology and Psychophysiology of Labor*, vol. 3 (1930), no. 5, pp. 374–384.

"The Mind, Consciousness, Unconsciousness." In *Elements of General Psychology*, 4th ed., pp. 48–61. Moscow: Extension Division of the Second Moscow State University, 1930.

"The Development of the Highest Patterns of Behavior in Childhood." Report to the First Meeting of Human Behavior, Jan. 28, 1930. In *Psychoneurological Sciences in the USSR*, pp. 138–139. Moscow-Leningrad: Medgiz, 1930.

"The Development of Consciousness in Childhood." Private archives of L. S. Vygotsky. Stenography.

"Sleep and Dreams." In *Elements of General Psychology,* pp. 62–75. Moscow: Extension Division of the Second Moscow State University, 1930.

"The Communist Reconstruction of Man." *Varnitso,* 1930, nos. 9–10, pp. 36–44.

"Structural Psychology." In *Main Trends in Contemporary Psychology* by L. S. Vygotsky and S. Gellershtein, pp. 84–125. Moscow-Leningrad: Government Publishing House, 1930.

"Eidetics." In *Main Trends in Contemporary Psychology* by L. S. Vygotsky and S. Gellershtein, pp. 178–205. Moscow-Leningrad: Government Publishing House, 1930.

"Experimental Investigation of the Highest Processes of Behavior." Report to the First Meeting for Studying Human Behavior, Jan. 28, 1930. In *Psychoneurological Sciences in the USSR.* Moscow-Leningrad: Medgiz, 1930.

1931

Buhler, C., et al. *The Social-Psychological Study of the Child During the First Year of Life.* L. S. Vygotsky, ed. Moscow-Leningrad: Medgiz, 1931. (With A. R. Luria.)

"Report of the Reactological Discussion, 1931." Archives of the Institute of General and Pedagogical Psychology, Academy of Pedagogical Sciences, USSR, fol. 82, vol. I, pp. 5–15. Stenography (corrected by L. S. Vygotsky).

The Diagnosis of Development and Pedological Clinics for Difficult Children. Moscow: Publishing House of the Experimental Defectology Institute, 1936.

"The History of the Development of Higher Psychological Functions." In *Development of Higher Psychological Functions* by L. S. Vygotsky, pp. 13–223. Moscow: Academy of Pedogogical Sciences, RSFSR, 1960.

"The Question of Compensatory Processes in the Development of the Retarded Child." Report to the Conference of the Workers of Auxiliary Schools, Leningrad, May 23, 1931. Private archives of L. S. Vygotsky. Stenography, 48 pp.

"Problems of Pedology and Related Sciences." *Pedology,* 1931, no. 3, pp. 52–58.

"The Collective as a Factor of Development in the Abnormal Child." In *Problems of Defectology,* 1931, nos. 1–2, pp. 8–17; no. 3, pp. 3–18.

"Thinking." *The Great Soviet Encyclopedia,* 1931, vol. XIX, cols. 414–426.

The Pedology of Teenagers. Lectures 9–16. Moscow-Leningrad: Extension Division of the Second Moscow State University, 1931.

"Practical Activity and Thinking in the Development of the Child in Connection with a Problem of Politechnism." Private archives of L. S. Vygotsky. Manuscript, 4 pp.

Foreword to *Development of Memory* by A. N. Leontiev. Moscow-Leningrad: Uchpedgiz, 1931.

Foreword to *Essay on the Behavior and Education of the Deaf-Mute Child* by Y. K. Zvelfel. Moscow-Leningrad: Uchpedgiz, 1931.

The Psychological Dictionary. Moscow: Uchpedgiz, 1931. (With B. E. Varshava.)

"Psychotechnics and Pedology." Report to the Meeting of the Communist Academy, Nov. 21, 1930. Archives of the Institute of General and Pedagogical Psychology, Academy of Pedagogical Sciences, USSR, fol. 82, vol. I, no. 3, pp. 23–57.

1932

"The Problem of Creativity in Actors." In *The Psychology of the Stage Feelings of an Actor* by P. M. Jakobson, pp. 197–211. Moscow: Government Publishing House, 1936.

"Toward a Psychology of Schizophrenia." *Soviet Neuropathology, Psychiatry and Psychohygiene,* vol. 1 (1932), no. 8, pp. 352–361.

"Toward a Psychology of Schizophrenia." In *Contemporary Problems of Schizophrenia,* pp. 19–28. Moscow: Medgiz, 1933.

"Lectures on Psychology." Leningrad Pedagogical Institute, March-April 1932. Archives of the Leningrad Pedagogical Institute. Stenography. Also in *Development of Higher Psychological Functions,* pp. 235–363. Moscow: Academy of Pedagogical Sciences, RSFSR, 1960.

"Infancy." Private archives of L. S. Vygotsky. Manuscript, 78 pp.

Foreword to *Education and Teaching of the Retarded Child* by E. K. Gracheva. Moscow-Leningrad: Uchpedgiz, 1932.

Foreword to *Development of Memory* by A. N. Leontiev. Moscow, 1932. (With A. N. Leontiev.)

"The Problem of Development of the Child in the Research of Arnold Gesell." In *Education and Childhood* by A. Gesell, pp. 3–14. Moscow-Leningrad: Uchpedgiz, 1932.

"Problem of the Speech and Thinking of the Child in the Teachings of Piaget." In *Language and Thought of the Child* by J. Piaget, pp. 3–54. Moscow-Leningrad: Uchpedgiz, 1932.

"Early Childhood." Lecture, Leningrad Pedagogical Institute, Dec. 15, 1932. Archives of the Leningrad Pedagogical Institute. Stenography, 50 pp.

"Contemporary Directions in Psychology." Report to the Communist Academy, June 26, 1932. In *Development of Higher Psychological Functions* by L. S. Vygotsky, pp. 458–481. Moscow: Academy of Pedagogical Sciences, RSFSR, 1960.

1933

"Introductory Lecture about Age-Psychology." The Central House of Art Education of Children, Dec. 19, 1933. Archives of the Leningrad Pedagogical Institute. Stenography, 34 pp.

"Dynamics of Mental Development of School Children in Connection with Education." Report to the Meeting of the Department of Defectology of Bubnov Pedagogical Institute, Dec. 23, 1933. In *Mental Development of Children during Education* by L. S. Vygotsky, pp. 33–52. Moscow-Leningrad: Government Publishing House, 1935.

"Preschool Age." Lecture, Leningrad Pedagogical Institute, Dec. 13–14, 1933. Private archives of L. S. Vygotsky. Stenography, 15 pp.

"Play and Its Role in the Psychological Development of the Child." Lecture, Leningrad Pedagogical Institute, 1933. *Problems of Psychology,* 1966, no. 6, pp. 62–76.

"Questions about the Dynamics of Development of the Intellect of the Normal and Abnormal Child." Lecture, Bubnov Pedagogical Institute, Dec. 23, 1933. Private archives of L. S. Vygotsky. Stenography.

"Crisis of the First Year of Life." Lecture, Leningrad Pedagogical Institute. Archives of the Leningrad Pedagogical Institute. Stenography, 37 pp.

"Critical Ages." Lecture, Leningrad Pedagogical Institute, June 26, 1933. Archives of the Leningrad Pedagogical Institute. Manuscript, 15 pp.

"The Negative Phase of Adolescence." Lecture, Leningrad Pedagogical Institute, June 26, 1933. Archives of the Leningrad Pedagogical Institute. Manuscript, 17 pp.

"Study of Schoolwork in School Children." Report to the Leningrad Pedagogical Institute, Jan. 31, 1933. Private archives of L. S. Vygotsky. Stenography.

"Pedological Study of the Pedagogical Process." Report to the Experimental Defectological Institute, March 17, 1933. In *Mental Development of Children during Education* by L. S. Vygotsky, pp. 116–134. Moscow-Leningrad: Uchpedgiz, 1935.

"Adolescence." Lecture, Leningrad Pedagogical Institute, June 25, 1933. Archives of the Leningrad Pedagogical Institute. Stenography, 19 pp.

"Pedology of Preschool Age." Lecture, Leningrad Pedagogical Institute, Jan. 31, 1933. Archives of the Leningrad Pedagogical Institute. Stenography, 16 pp.

Foreword to *Difficult Children in Schoolwork* by L. V. Zankov, M. S. Pevsner, and V. F. Shmidt. Moscow-Leningrad: Uchpedgiz, 1933.

"Problems of Age: Play." Concluding speech to the Seminar of the Leningrad Pedagogical Institute, March 23, 1933. Archives of the Leningrad Pedagogical Institute. Stenography, 39 pp.

"Problems of Development." Lecture, Leningrad Pedagogical Institute, Nov. 27, 1933. Archives of the Leningrad Pedagogical Institute. Stenography, 17 pp.

"The Problem of Consciousness." Report after the speech of A. R. Luria on Dec. 5 and 9, 1933. In *Psychology of Grammar,* pp. 178–196. Moscow: Moscow State University, 1968.

"Development of Common Sense and Scientific Ideas during School Age." Report to the Scientific Conference, Leningrad Pedagogical Institute, May 20, 1933. In *Mental Development of Children during Education,* pp. 96–115. Moscow-Leningrad: Uchpedgiz, 1935.

"Study of Emotions." Private archives of L. S. Vygotsky, 1933. Manuscript. 555 pp. Also "The Study of Emotions in the Light of Contemporary Psychoneurology." *Questions of Philosophy,* 1970, no. 6, pp. 110–130. See also, "Two Directions in the Comprehension of the Nature of Emotions in Foreign Psychology in the beginning of the Twentieth Century." *Problems of Psychology,* 1968, no. 2, pp. 149–156.

1934

"Dementia during Pick's Disease." *Soviet Neuropathology, Psychiatry, Psychohygiene,* vol. 3 (1934), no. 6, pp. 97–136. (With G. V. Birenbaum and N. V. Samukhin.)

"Development of Scientific Ideas during Childhood." In *The Development of Scientific Ideas of School Children* by Zh. I. Shif, pp. 3–17. Moscow-Leningrad: Uchpedgiz, 1935.

"Infancy and Early Age." Lecture, Leningrad Pedagogical Institute, Feb. 23, 1934. Archives of the Leningrad Pedagogical Institute. Stenography, 24 pp.

Thought and Language. Moscow-Leningrad: Sozekgiz, 1934.

"The Thinking of School Children." Lecture, Leningrad Pedagogical Institute, May 3, 1934. Archives of the Leningrad Pedagogical Institute. Stenography, 11 pp.

Fundamentals of Pedology. Moscow: Second Moscow Medical Institute, 1934.

"Adolescence." Lecture, Leningrad Pedagogical Institute, March 25, 1934. Archives of the Leningrad Pedagogical Institute. Stenography.

"Problems of Age." Private archives of L. S. Vygotsky. Manuscript, 95 pp. Also in *Problems of Psychology,* 1972, no. 2, pp. 114–123.

"Problems of Education and Mental Development in School Age." In *Mental Development of Children during Education* by L. S. Vygotsky, pp. 3–19. Moscow-Leningrad: Uchpedgiz, 1935.

"Problem of Development in Structural Psychology." In *Fundamentals of Psychological Development* by K. Koffka, pp. ix–lxi. Moscow-Leningrad: Sozekgiz, 1934.

"Problem of Development and Destruction of the Higher Psychological Functions." In *Development of Higher Psychological Functions* by L. S. Vygotsky, pp. 364–383. Moscow: Academy of Pedagogical Sciences, RSFSR, 1960. (Vygotsky's last report, prepared one month before his death.)

"Psychology and Teaching of Localization." In *Reports of the First Ukranian Meeting of Neuropathologists and Psychiatrists,* pp. 34–41. Kharkov, 1934.

"Dementia during Pick's Disease." Private archives of L. S. Vygotsky, 1934. Manuscript, 4 pp.

Fascism in Psychoneurology. Moscow-Leningrad: Biomedgiz, 1934. (With V. A. Giljarovsky et al.)

"School Age." Private archives of D. B. Elkonin, 1934. Manuscript, 42 pp.

"School Age." Lecture, Leningrad Pedagogical Institute, Feb. 23, 1934. Archives of the Leningrad Pedagogical Institute. Stenography, 61 pp.

"Experimental Investigation of the Teaching of New Speech Reflexes by the Method of Attachment with Complexes." Private archives of L. S. Vygotsky. Manuscript.

1935

"Education and Development during School Age." Report to the National

Conference of Preschool Education. In *Mental Development of Children during Education,* pp. 20–32. Moscow-Leningrad: Uchpedgiz, 1935.

"Problem of Dementia." In *The Retarded Child,* pp. 7–34. Moscow-Leningrad: Uchpedgiz, 1935.

The Retarded Child. L. S. Vygotsky, ed. Moscow-Leningrad: Uchpedgiz, 1935.

Works of Various Years

Pedology of Youth: Features of the Behavior of the Teenager. Lessons 6–9. Moscow: Extension Division of the Faculty of Education, Second Moscow State University.

"Problem of the Cultural Development of the Child." Private archives of L. S. Vygotsky. Manuscript, 81 pp.

"The Blind Child." Private archives of L. S. Vygotsky. Manuscript, 3 pp.

Difficult Childhood. Moscow: Extension Division of the Faculty of Education, Second Moscow State University.

IN ENGLISH

"The Principles of Social Education of Deaf and Dumb Children in Russia." In *International Conference on the Education of the Deaf,* pp. 227–237. London, 1925.

"The Problem of the Cultural Development of the Child." *Journal of Genetic Psychology,* 1929, vol. 36, pp. 415–434.

"Thought in Schizophrenia." *Archives of Neurological Psychiatry,* 1934, vol. 31.

"Thought and Speech." *Psychiatry,* 1939, vol. 2, pp. 29–54. Rpt. in S. Saporta, ed., *Psycholinguistics: A Book of Readings,* pp. 509–537. New York: Holt, Rinehart and Winston, 1961.

Thought and Language. Cambridge: MIT Press and Wiley, 1962. (Originally published in Russian in 1934.)

"Psychology and Localization of Functions." *Neuropsychologia,* 1965, vol. 3, pp. 381–386. (Originally published in Russian in 1934.)

"Development of the Higher Mental Functions." In A. Leontiev, A. Luria, and A. Smirnov, eds., *Psychological Research in the USSR,* vol. I, pp. 11–46. Progress Publishing, 1966. (Abridged.)

"Play and Its Role in the Mental Development of the Child." *Soviet Psychology,* 1967, vol. 3. (Vygotsky memorial issue. Includes preface by J. S. Bruner and articles by Soviet psychologists Luria, Davydov, El'konin, Gal'perin, and Zaporozhetz. Article based on 1933 lecture.)

The Psychology of Art. Cambridge: MIT Press, 1971. (Collected writings of literary and art criticism spanning several decades.)

"Spinoza's Theory of the Emotions in Light of Contemporary Psychoneurology." *Soviet Studies in Philosophy,* 1972, vol. 10, pp. 362–382.

Index

Ach, N., 67

Action: repetition of, 22; purposeful, symbolic representations of, 37; –meaning ratio, 100–101; play and, 129. *See also* Gestures; Linguistics; Play; Symbolism

Adaptation: and children's adaptive behavior, 22, 24; sign and tool use as means of, 53, 55, 123, 124, 127 (*see also* Signs, use of; Tools, use of); and adaptability of animals, 60, 132 (*see also* Animals)

Adolescence, *see* Age

Age: "chimpanzee," 21 (*see also* Animals); and practical intelligence/ thought, 21–22, 23, 24, 51, 79–80, 97; and speech, 25–26, 28, 29, 32, 62; and perception, 31–32, 33, 97, 98; and choice behavior/response, 33, 70; and color-task errors, 41–45; infancy, and roots of cultural behavior, 46; and memory, 47–49, 50, 56, 139n.3; adolescence, 61, 83, 104, 129; mental, 85–88, 89; and play, 92–94, 102, 104, 111, 129; and situational constraints, 96, 98–99; and action vs. meaning, 100–101; and graphic depiction, 108 (*see also* Gestures); and symbolic notation, 109–112, 113, 114, 115; and reading, writing, 117; and imagination, 129. *See also* Child development; Linguistics; Maturation; Tests and testing

All-Union Institute of Experimental Medicine (USSR), 16

America, *see* United States

Analysis: developmental, 8, 61–62, 65 (*see also* Behavior); of process vs. objects (experimental-developmental), 61–62, 65; explanatory vs. descriptive (genotypic vs. phenotypic), 62–63, 65, 67, 68; aim of, 63, 64, 65; introspective, 63, 65–68; "fossilized" behavior and, 63–65, 68; of choice reaction, 66–69 (*see also* Choice behavior and responses); of teaching, 79; of educational process, 90–91

Animals: study of, linked with human studies, 2–3, 4, 6, 60, 122, 124; and use of tools, 7, 22, 23, 24, 88; Köhler's ape studies, 20–23 (passim), 25, 28, 31, 37, 88; and child–ape comparisons; 20–23, 26, 28, 34, 36, 37; and sign use, 23, 39; and linguistics, 23, 136n.7; and perception, 31, 32–33, 34, 35, 36, 37; and attention, 36; and voluntary activity, 37; and memory aids, 39, 51, 127; and internalization, 57; and adaptability/adaptation, 60, 132; and learning, 88; and imagination, 93, 129

Aphasia, 9, 22. *See also* Linguistics

Aristotle, 53

Attention: in problem solving (of child), 35–36; role of signs in, 40; development of, 57; voluntary and involuntary ("secondary," primary"), 64